THE
TOP
200
WEB SITES FOR
MARKETING

The Top 200 Web Sites
CD ROM + Guides

This series of interactive CD ROMs with accompanying Guides provides access to the *best quality* business information sites on the Net. Forget those hours of frustrating searching. Now the work has been done for you. Illustra's team of researchers has spent countless hours scrutinizing thousands of Web sites to select only those that are truly relevant and useful to your specific needs.

Available so far in this new series:

- The Top 200 Web Sites on E-Commerce
- The Top 200 Web Sites for Marketing
- The Top 200 Web Sites for Personal Finance
- The Top 200 Web Sites for Small Business

Each CD ROM features:

- fast access to the selected sites;
- a fully featured Web browser;
- free online information updates.

Each accompanying Guide gives general advice on how to make best use of the Internet as an information resource, and detailed descriptions and ratings of each selected site.

Designed to save busy people valuable time and money, each CD ROM and Guide together provide a powerful interactive business tool.

The author of *The Top 200 Web Sites for Marketing*, Mark Walker, is a marketing and communications consultant with over ten years' marketing experience. For five years he has been a director of the Sussex Community Internet Project, one of the leading agencies concerned with offering training and support to community groups.

THE
TOP
200
WEB SITES FOR
MARKETING

Mark Walker

INSTITUTE OF DIRECTORS

KOGAN
PAGE

First published in 2000

Kogan Page Limited
120 Pentonville Road
London N1 9JN
UK

Kogan Page US
163 Central Avenue, Suite 2
Dover NH 03820
USA

This book has been endorsed by the Institute of Directors.

The endorsement is given to selected Kogan Page books which the IoD recognizes as being of specific interest to its members and providing them with up-to-date, informative and practical resources for creating business success. Kogan Page books endorsed by the IoD represent the most authoritative guidance available on a wide range of subjects including management, finance, marketing, training and HR.

The views expressed in this book are those of the author and are not necessarily the same as those of the Institute of Directors.

British Library Cataloguing in Publication Data

A CIP record for this book is available from the British Library.

ISBN 0 7494 3269 1

Typeset by Saxon Graphics Ltd, Derby
Printed and bound in Great Britain by Bell & Bain Ltd, Glasgow

Contents

1 Explore marketing Web sites with this guide   **1**

How we select and rate the Top 200 Web sites   3

2 Using the Internet for business   **7**

So what's all the fuss about?   7

The value of the Internet to business users   8

User driven, not technology driven   9

Essential business benefits of the Internet — a summary   9

How can good-quality information be free on the Web?   10

Why you shouldn't ignore the Internet   11

How we deal with commercial sites or vendors   12

3 Web site types – a user's guide   **14**

Seven types of Web site   14

4 Beyond the Web – e-mail and newsgroups   **22**

E-mail is easy   22

Are you getting the most from your e-mail?   23

Newsgroups   27

5 Marketing and the Internet   **30**

Introduction   30

General resources   30

Advertising   35

6 Direct marketing and international marketing 40

Direct marketing 40
International marketing 45
The European Union 52

7 Internet marketing 54

8 Marketing news and events 63

News and magazines 63
Events and conferences 66

9 Marketing research and public relations 70

Marketing research 70
Public relations 74

The Top 200 Web sites for marketing 77

Business essentials 77
General marketing 83
Advertising 88
Direct marketing 92
Internet marketing 96
International marketing 101
Marketing research 105
Public relations 110
News and magazines 112
Events and conferences 116

Index 118

1

Explore marketing Web sites with this guide

The Internet is an exciting new tool for marketing products and services. It offers a dynamic and sophisticated means of conducting effective communication both with customers and with other marketing people. The Web is packed full of marketing-related information, ranging from news and general resources to material on public relations and direct marketing techniques. You can use the Net to trawl for information on competitors, prospects, partners or creditworthiness. It offers you a marketing research tool with a global reach; you can do list purchasing at the click of a mouse; and of course, it is the natural home of information and resources about Internet marketing, including effective e-mail marketing and how to create your own online strategy.

Before reading further, please note: this book is **not** a guide to how to do marketing via the Internet. From this guide you can expect:

- Fast access (via the CD ROM) to high-quality marketing Web sites.

- A critical overview of marketing and business-oriented Web sites that are currently available online, and pointers that will help you become more Internet literate.

- A guide that concentrates on the **content** of Web sites and its usefulness to a marketing audience that is not obsessed by the technology.

- Tips on how to get more from the Internet as an information resource.

- A guide that focuses on using the World Wide Web (WWW), although you will find a section on e-mail and newsgroups.

What you won't get from this book:

- A manual that will tell you how to become a marketing (or Internet marketing) expert. If you want that sort of guide, put this book down **now**! This guide offers an overview of what information resources you can expect to find **on the Internet** in a particular subject area. The guide won't instruct you in the subject but it will give you access to a range of useful Web sites from which you will be able to learn a great deal in your chosen area of interest.

- Any pretence that every marketing Web site that ever existed has been scoured in the process of writing this book. That's about as realistic as someone claiming to have catalogued and read every book in the world. Thousands of Web sites have been evaluated in the process of making this book, and every site undergoes the rigorous research process outlined below. We can guarantee that each guide features a hand-picked selection of Web sites that you will find useful.

- Detailed instructions on how to build a cracking Web site, though we do include sites that may help you to do this. Our aim is to promote the Web as an information resource, and is therefore aimed at marketing professionals who want to improve their Web skills.

Don't think this guide is going to stay up to date unless you regularly update it. We've all heard the clichés about a day being a long time on the Net. It's certainly true that what is currently available on the

Internet that is of use to a marketing audience will have changed within a couple of months. Once you have bought the guide, updates can be easily obtained by visiting the Illustra Research Web site. Check it out for yourself by clicking the Illustra button within the guide.

How we select and rate the Top 200 Web sites in this guide

Illustra Research has devised its own procedures to locate, select and evaluate Web sites, and the same criteria are applied across each of the different guides in the Top 200 series. We have examined a wide range of methodologies that other people, often university librarians, have devised to judge the quality of information on the Internet, and have incorporated these into our own system.

All the reviewed and rated Web sites in this book have been individually examined and measured against our twin criteria, **relevance** and **ease of use**. We use these criteria to present a shortlist of the very best sites our team of authors and researchers have found over months of searching and evaluation.

Underlying our criteria is one all-important factor – the extent to which a Web site does, or does not, meet the needs of a particular group of users. We are not trying to establish a universal quality standard, or a 'Good Housekeeping seal of approval' system. We have designed our system of selection and evaluation in order to present sites that we think our target group of users is going to find valuable as sources of information.

But can you trust our judgements? Doesn't any review or rating system in the end depend on personal taste? How can a star rating sum up the value of a Web site? Responding to these concerns we have developed a two-step method for identifying sites worth sharing. Our authors have employed this evaluation process and we include details to show how demanding we have been when choosing the sites for the guide.

Step one: establishing threshold criteria

With thousands of potential sites to sift through we established our baseline for inclusion. Using our two criteria, relevance and ease of use, we designed a checklist of those attributes a Web site must possess before we consider recommending it.

Relevance

Here we think about the accuracy and credibility of the site's content. Is the purpose and scope of the site clear, or does it have a hidden agenda? Does the site undergo regular updates or revisions? Is there a physical address, or at least a phone number, to confirm the existence in the real world of those responsible for the site? Does it present information in a way that is sensitive to what marketing professionals are likely to want?

Ease of use

Here we look at the design and the navigation facilities. We consider how friendly they are for a newcomer to the Web – someone short of time but hungry for information. What is the general appearance of the site? Is the text easy to read? Are the links appropriate and well described? We think that interactivity is essential for an effective site, you should be able to ask questions, carry out transactions and generally use the information in a more active way that simply reading words off a screen. So the sites we rate highly offer much more than simply an e-mail address for communication with their users.

Step two: awarding a star rating

The star rating for relevance and ease of use provides a quick guide to what the site offers. Sites that satisfy the threshold criteria are measured on a scale of one to five. Here we distinguish what is good, what is better and what is truly outstanding. The key to the ratings is listed here in full.

Relevance

✪	This site offers basic, useful information.
✪✪	This site provides some useful information plus some expert insight or value.
✪✪✪	A comprehensive site with authoritative information and resources.
✪✪✪✪	An excellent, authoritative site with features that make it an indispensable tool.
✪✪✪✪✪	The very best of its kind to be found at present. A 'must see'.

Ease of use

✪	An accessible, easy to navigate interface with limited interactive features.
✪✪	An interface with some interactive features that enrich user experience.
✪✪✪	An interface that conveys a high level of design and usability in most areas.
✪✪✪✪	An interface that conveys a high level of design and usability in all areas.
✪✪✪✪✪	The best in its class – redefines the current standard of excellence.

A one-star rating for relevance indicates that the site is well worth a visit for basic information, some of which may be unique to the organization that runs it and will not be found elsewhere. As each of our guides is aimed at a particular group of business users, all the sites recommended in them have a value; if we have found a site that we think is useful, it will be in the guide. For this reason there are no zero scores for relevance in *The Top 200 Web Sites for Marketing* – what would be the point? Some sites may have a zero score for ease of use however. In such cases the standard of information contained on the site compensates for its poor design. We trust that in time, perhaps even by the time you come to visit the site, improvements will have been made and the usability of the site will match the standard of its content.

Rapid change is one of the Web's greatest strengths as an information source and we appreciate that sites can alter between visits. We are committed to constantly reviewing and re-evaluating the contents of our guides. For this reason all our reviews carry the date the site was assessed. A site that is regularly updated and has satisfied our demand for accuracy, credibility and usability should, by its nature, maintain a high standard. But your comments and contributions are invaluable. If you think our reviews don't match your views, it may be because the site has changed, so please do let us know if you think you've found a site that we should include – visit the Illustra Web site by clicking the Illustra button, then click on **My Sites**.

2

Using the Internet for business

So what's all the fuss about?

The rise of the Internet is seemingly unstoppable. Media coverage reminds us daily that the Internet and the Web are going to transform how people live and do business. We are urged to go online and get Internet literate. Bookshops are adorned with guides to becoming 'Net savvy'– but have you wondered what all the fuss is about? Have *you* noticed that using the Internet can be disappointing or even worse, a positively frustrating experience?

The Internet for many people is an **information jungle,** and the sheer scale of information available is overwhelming. Search engines offer a crude and inadequate tool for information searching, since no quality assurance system operates. Most searches made with search engines return a vast number of Web sites, with no guarantee that the information turned up will be useful or relevant.

Business users don't have time or money to waste doing this sort of thankless searching. What you need is access to high-quality Web sites oriented to the specific needs of a business audience. However, when you use the Web, you end up 'ploughing' through thousands of largely irrelevant search results; it's like being given an unreliable and gargantuan guide to the world when you just want solid and dependable information about a weekend break in Lisbon.

To make it worse, half the sites you come across are appalling, out of date or 'under construction'. How many businesses do you know who would mail out a sales brochure with blank pages saying 'not yet written'? There is no quality control or equivalent of 'refuse disposal' on the Web, and again and again you will come across 'detritus' sites, created and then abandoned, filled with inaccurate and incomplete information. Using the Web feels more like 'grubbing around' in a skip than being on an information superhighway, and you can waste half the morning on unsuccessful Internet searches. So what *is* all the fuss about?

The value of the Internet to business users

Despite these familiar difficulties, there *is* useful information available on the Web, which *can* save UK business users time and money. For example, did you know that British business users can currently use the Web to do all the following activities without any payment:

- Check phone bills and amend discount offers.
- Print out detailed street maps of anywhere in the UK by typing in a postcode.
- Set up e-mail groups, which enable them to keep in contact with business colleagues who don't share a computer network with them.
- Compare house prices, crime rates or council tax bills with those in other areas or with the national average.
- Compare water, gas and electricity bills with what they might have paid with a different supplier.
- Find businesses, UK phone numbers, UK postcodes, company information – all for free!

Apart from these 'business essentials' that anyone will find useful (which are of course all in the guide), there is specific information out there relevant to your business. Whether you need to know about employment law, job vacancies, training opportunities, stock market quotations or export markets, there is often timely information that can be much easier to obtain than it is in print – provided you know where to look. However, it takes time and some degree of familiarity with the Web to locate these useful sites, and neither of these is easy for over-stretched business users to acquire.

The guide saves time and effort by offering an overview of a particular subject of relevance to business users, and by providing fast access via the CD ROM to some of the most useful sites in that area. Each guide is packed with reviews of Web sites that have been hand-picked for their usefulness and quality. The research is invaluable for beginners and experienced users alike, since it takes all the hassle out of Internet use, with no more hours spent, bleary eyed, 'ploughing' through hundreds of irrelevant search findings.

User driven, not technology driven

The solid research behind the guides is based on a clear understanding of how the Internet works as channel of communication and information, not just as a technology. You will have already found that most guides to the Internet tell you more than you ever want to know about the technology, but less than you need to know about what is out there. The guides in The Top 200 series tell you how to *use* the technology, and focus on the specific needs of groups of users. For example, we know the Internet is good for British business users for the following reasons:

Essential business benefits of the Internet – a summary

- The Internet provides access to a wealth of up-to-date information from a variety of sources, which can be invaluable for businesses when information changes quickly, or when comparisons need to be made, eg for purchasing.

- The Internet is a cost-effective channel for communication, especially in global terms.

- It provides a good way to network and generate business that goes far beyond one's physical geographic reach.

- It gives small companies the opportunity to compete on the same footing as larger companies, since they can sell on a global scale without the large overheads of a shop-front presence or having to embark on costly paper-based marketing campaigns.

- The interactive features of the Web can be used to create more sophisticated and attractive product delivery channels for consumers, eg through providing searchable databases on product lines or by providing links to other sites. This benefits vendors *and* consumers.

- The Internet offers access to free, good-quality information which cannot be obtained as easily or as conveniently from other sources.

How can good-quality information be free on the Web?

This is because many organizations have jumped on the online bandwagon but haven't worked out yet how to make people pay for this information. On commercial sites, revenue is usually acquired by following an advertising model, and because they want to attract people, and therefore keep advertisers happy, they offer services and features including free information that they hope will pull in visitors. This might change with the development of new kinds of online payment systems, but at the moment it makes much of the free information on the Web extremely valuable – if you can find it, of course.

The other reason why valuable information is available on the Web without charge is that many of the information providers are governmental or non-profit-making bodies. They offer information as a function of their responsibilities to the public.

Why you shouldn't ignore the Internet

You may be bored by all the hype around the Internet. However, there are some important reasons why businesses should not ignore the Internet. For example, one reason why it is currently difficult to locate good-quality sites is that hype and excitement about the Web has led to companies and organizations rushing to 'get online'. Consequently, many current sites have no obvious value or usefulness and have been thrown up by companies desperate to carve out a Web presence. They are created without enough consideration or awareness as to what makes a valuable or useful site. They are usually ill conceived and poorly designed 'corporate brochures', so it is not surprising that their pages are frustrating to users (see Chapter 3).

However, as the technology matures, and the use and design of Web sites becomes more sophisticated, it is likely that many of the more hopeless ones will get 'weeded out', and Internet users will become more adept at recognizing styles and categories of sites. These more literate Internet business users will be significantly advantaged over individuals who have shunned the Internet because they think it is full of rubbish, and have yet to acquire any familiarity with it; or users like those TV viewers who don't recognize the distinction between soap operas and news broadcasts. Since the Internet is here to stay, some degree of Internet literacy is necessary just to be able to operate in the new channels of communication and information that have been created for business by the Web. Even if you have other people in your organization whose job it is to 'ferret out' the necessary information, it will help you considerably if you know what can be done with the Internet – and can judge for example whether a particular piece of research really would take a week to complete!

Key points

- Don't ignore the Internet because you think it'll go away – it won't!
- Don't allow yourself to be swayed or panicked by the hype.
- Recognize the strengths of the Internet for business as well as its weaknesses.
- Use this guide to begin to make yourself more Internet literate.

How we deal with commercial sites or vendors

In this book and on the CD ROM, you will find reviews of vendors' sites in a range of product areas. These sites have been included because they are good examples of their kind, eg e-commerce-enabled sites, or they may offer information or additional features that set them aside from other vendors' sites of their type. Most straightforward commercial sites, which use the Internet solely as a promotional medium (and are described in Chapter 3 as 'corporate brochure' sites), have **not** been included in this book. For example, we have made no attempt to include a complete listing of the Web sites of, say, firms who repair computers. One reason is that, if you live in Ashford, it will not help you to have to 'wade' through sites of firms in Barnsley. Another is that there are good sites *on the Internet* that do exactly this. You may have heard of Yahoo! or Yellow Pages, but have you heard of Scoot? (see Business essentials).

Wherever possible we have tried to find sites that help you find the commercial products and services you are looking for. 'Corporate brochure' sites perform a valuable function (if you are sure you want information about that company and they provide it). What the Internet does really well is deliver up-to-the-minute information from the databases that lie behind the Web sites. We have included directories of vendors that are comprehensive, easily searchable and maintained on a daily or weekly basis. We have excluded those 'directories' where firms included have to pay, those that are patchy in coverage, are not maintained, or are impossibly difficult to use.

3

Web site types – a user's guide

We have all learnt to recognize types of television programmes, for example, what a documentary looks like as opposed to a soap opera, or what to expect from the *Nine O'Clock News*, but it is not quite so easy with Web sites. The Internet is a new medium and Web sites often cross over several forms and styles, borrowing from newspapers, advertising and television amongst many others. What's more, they are changing all the time.

However, there *are* recognizable characteristics that can help you identity what you can expect from a Web site. Getting familiar with these signs can help you pinpoint what type of Web page you've just stumbled on to and help you establish quickly whether it is going to be of any use to you. Read on for an introduction to the fascinating art of Web site spotting.

Seven types of Web site

Type one: the 'corporate brochure'

This type of site reflects the spectacularly boring efforts of a company that has usually just taken the text and images from its corporate brochure and put them online.

You will often find that such sites were constructed in a fit of enthusiasm; usually by firms who had just discovered the Web and thought they should have a Web presence. They had no clue about why or what they should do with it. In most cases, they simply transferred their promotional literature on to the site; now they wonder why no-one ever visits it. As a consequence of this failure, and the subsequent loss of initial enthusiasm, such sites can fall into a state of chronic disrepair with little updating or maintenance. Others are updated but remain tedious.

You can recognize these sites by the fact they look like corporate brochures – typically the home page will feature glossy photographs or logos, and it is always the same thing on the 'menu': pages on Services (sales pitch) About Us (historically slanted sales pitch) and Products (relentless, full-frontal sales pitch). You won't find e-commerce on a corporate brochure site, or any interactive features. You may be lucky and find an e-mail address, but don't be surprised if you don't get a reply when you use it.

You won't find any examples of corporate brochures in the guide as they don't satisfy our criteria for what makes a site useful. But you will find directory sites with links to many of these sites. If you want specific information about a particular company, then 'corporate brochure' sites can be useful.

Type 2: the 'labour of love'

The amateurish layout, the background that makes it harder to read the text, even the use of standard clipart are all characteristics of a 'labour of love' Web site; usually created by an individual who is an obsessive enthusiast, who wants to share his or her passion or knowledge about a subject with the rest of the world. These individuals collect links to absolutely everything they can find on the Internet, and sometimes add their own comments to the lists of links.

Whilst most 'labours of love' are the work of hobbyists, you will come across business-oriented Internet sites that are 'labours of love' and they *can* be very useful and informative. You need to exercise your discretion and decide for yourself. Often, like many works of art, 'labours of love' are left unfinished or are even abandoned, so don't presume the material presented is up to date or even accurate.

The following site, which deals with cryptography, is an example of a 'labour of love' that is genuinely useful to e-commerce specialists with a deep interest in security matters.

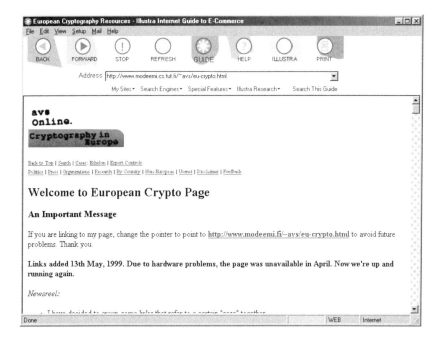

Type three: the 'flashy Flash'

The supreme example of the triumph of style over content, 'flashy Flash' sites tend to be hosted or created by designers or new media consultancies who want to show off their use of new media technologies (especially Macromedia's Flash animation package). Look out for intricate graphics, fancy dissolves and all things animated. The giveaway of a 'flashy Flash' site is a home page with something running across the screen for no obvious reason.

'Flashy Flash' sites can be bandwidth-hungry and tediously slow to download if you are working on a slow connection via a dial-up modem, or during peak use times. The best of these sites should give you the option to switch off the animation and some will require plug-ins (such as Shockwave) before you can even get into them.

We've no examples of this type in the guide. They didn't meet our criteria because the technology intrudes so much that the content is pushed aside (or not there in the first place). But there *is* Flash animation on some of the sites in the guide; used properly it can make informative sites interesting and even entertaining.

Type four: the news site or 'cluttered portal'

The news format is becoming increasingly popular on the Internet since it uses conventions of magazine and newspaper publishing to make Web sites attractive and familiar to users. On the left-hand side of the news site Web page there is typically a navigation menu, in the centre is regularly changed news copy, and on the right is a list of sponsors or links to other editions or publications. Using the news format prompts readers to recognize the site as a publication with changing text, and therefore encourages them to revisit, in the same way an individual might subscribe to a newspaper or magazine. News sites are often produced by offline publishers (such as the *Financial Times*) and focus on a specific interest area (as ZDNet does) or audience (as a trade journal would).

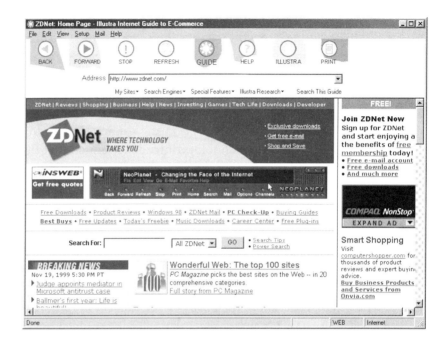

News sites can be well designed and pleasant to use. However, over-excitable site designers can try to stick too many menu options or links on them, hence the 'cluttered portal' phenomenon – a serious trial for the eyes. This problem is further magnified when 8pt type has been used by a designer in a effort to squeeze as much text into as small a space as possible.

News sites tend to be most useful if you want to browse in a particular subject area, rather than when you have a particular query or piece of information to look up. However, some people don't like browsing Internet sites and prefer to use paper publications, so it is really down to you to try out news sites for yourself.

Type five: the 'cunningly concealed commercial'

Like promotional features in magazines that ape the editorial layout of their 'host', these Web sites are trying to sell you something, but are pretending that it is not their main purpose. Common examples include Web sites presented as 'information resources' or 'directories', but you either have to pay to use them, the entries in the 'directory' are actually paid adverts, or the 'resources' are trying to selling you the services of a consultant.

A quick way to spot the 'cunningly concealed commercial' is to go to the About Us section on the home page and find out who has created and maintains the site. You shouldn't necessarily reject this sort of site but we all like to know where we stand. We have rejected them for The Top 200 series, but we have included some commercial sites that offer genuinely useful information *in addition to* a sales pitch.

Type six: the 'dull but worthy'

Mostly produced by public bodies, such as a trade association or your local council, these sites usually provide useful information but often give little thought to making accessing them a pleasurable or even straightforward process for their victim (the user).

Whilst the best can be accessible and sensibly organized, the worst will tell you what they do via a clunky and badly designed interface. Even more deadly is the tendency of some public body sites to feature numerous very boring documents on obscure aspects of regulatory or legislative procedure presented as pages and pages of dense text. The more advanced of these will allow you to download their documents, sometimes in PDF format, for which you need the (free) Adobe Acrobat reader installed.

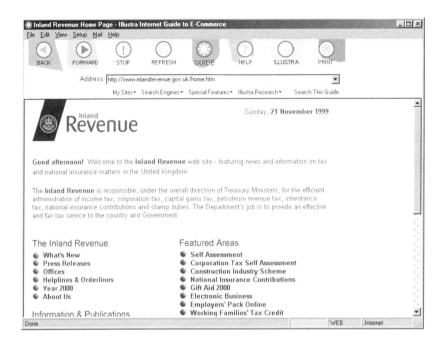

Public Web sites, such as the highly recommended Inland Revenue one featured above, are often useful as a first port of call when you need to deal with a particular agency, but public organizations usually lack the resources and/or imagination to develop truly innovative sites.

Type seven: the 'firm favourite'

These Web sites are sheer pleasure to use. They come in all shapes and sizes, but they are the ones you return to again and again. 'Firm favourites' usually exploit the interactive potential of the Web to the full. They are innovative, imaginative and offer something that really meets the needs of Internet users. On them you will find searchable databases, delivered via well-designed and intuitive interfaces. They provide access to features, services and information that cannot easily be found elsewhere *on* or even *off* the Web. It is this combination of excellent, fully interactive design *and* high-quality, genuinely useful information that makes a 'firm favourite' Web site.

Interestingly, it isn't just big players who can create these top-quality sites. In fact, it is often the simpler, more modest sites that exploit a clever idea with most flair and imagination. One example of this is found on the Multimap site. Here the linking of postcodes to online mapping makes it possible to provide a really useful service to anyone wanting to give directions to a particular place.

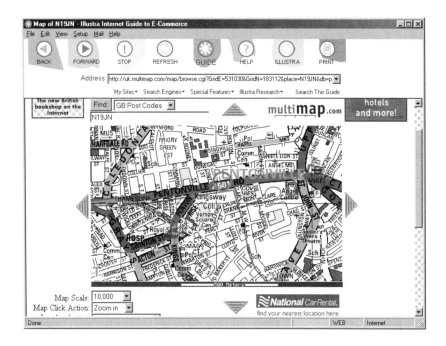

Sadly, 'firm favourites' are a rare occurrence on the Web at present. We can only hope that as Web site developers become more clued up, 'firm favourites' will become more common than the welcome exception. You will find such sites strongly featured in Business essentials.

4

Beyond the Web: e-mail and newsgroups

The hype around the Internet usually focuses upon the wonders of the World Wide Web, wowing us with 'cool' Web sites, the lure of e-commerce and the promised link-up with digital TV. But there are other tools available through the Net and it is worth considering their potential value before dashing off to surf the flashy attractions.

E-mail is easy

With the spotlight on 'dot.com' companies these days, e-mail seems very much the poor relation of the Internet. Yet electronic mail is a fantastically flexible tool for business people. It is cheap to use, easy to understand and has a lot of hidden abilities. Having been around for 30 years (since the birth of the Net) it is not subject to some of the technical changes that might force you to update your Web browser every three months.

For many people e-mail is the best reason for being on the Internet. It is a cheap, convenient means of communicating, whether across the office or around the globe. It can be used to keep in touch with people who are asleep when you're awake, to share news and information with hundreds of people at the same time, and it can offer access to customers, specialist information and new markets.

It can improve productivity, promote discussion amongst dispersed teams, notify you of an order or let a customer know that you've got a sale on. It is rapidly becoming an essential tool of modern business and sits neatly alongside the phone, letters and face-to-face meetings as part of the way to get things done.

Are you getting the most from your e-mail?

Whatever you think of the Internet, it is becoming increasingly difficult to avoid the use of e-mail. Anyone who can use a word processor can compose a message and send it to one, twenty or ten thousand people at the press of a button.

Despite fears about the growth of viruses and junk mail, the volume of e-mail traffic is growing even faster than the general growth of the Net. With the expanding convergence of e-mail with mobile phones and faxes, that level of expansion can only increase.

One-to-one e-mail

The starting point for e-mail is usually to see it as a substitute for an answerphone. I send you a message, which you receive when you check your mailbox. You compose a reply and send it back, so that I can pick it up when I next check my mail. It is an *asynchronous* means of communicating that has many benefits over the spoken word.

For a start, most people tend not to write in the same way as they speak. We tend to use whole sentences, for example, comprising complete words, and consider our message more carefully and for longer before committing it to paper, so a written message can often be clearer and more logically constructed than a spoken one. This helps both parties enormously. Replies can be more considered when you don't have to think instantly as you do on the telephone.

If I write you an e-mail, you can include my words in your reply. There is no need to spend ages explaining exactly what you're replying to, when you can copy my question back to me followed by a simple 'yes' or 'no'. You may want to copy my e-mail message into a word-processing document, or make some other use of it, without having to type anything yourself. You can forward it to someone else at a stroke, or copy others in on an exchange with a mutual colleague.

Of course a quick telephone call can be far more productive than a series of disjointed e-mails, and a chat over a pint is usually far more conducive to reaching an agreement than struggling to type with one finger. But as an option for one-to-one communication it offers advantages over phone, faxes and meetings that should not be underestimated.

One-to-many e-mail

The penetration of e-mail amongst the general population has created a huge impetus for communicating with lots of people in one go. The cost advantages over traditional mailing options are overwhelming, and the economy of scale is mind-blowing. Why send one message to one person by post for 20p when for about 5p (the current BT minimum charge) you can go online and send an e-mail to hundreds of people and for 10p send it to thousands.

'Spam'

The Internet community has long known of the potential benefits of mass mailing and has recognized that it also the potential to drown the Internet in a tide of e-mail. Because it is so difficult to regulate anything online, it has been left to Internet users themselves to seek to control the use of 'spam' – the name coined for the use of unsolicited e-mail sent to hundreds or thousands of people at the same time, usually through a mailing list or newsgroup that somebody else has created. It should be distinguished from targeted e-mail sent to a mailing list that you or your company have created.

If you need to know more about a term like 'spam' – and whether it did indeed originate from that Monty Python sketch – you can make use of the Writing aids section in Business essentials. The invaluable *Webopedia* also helps you out:

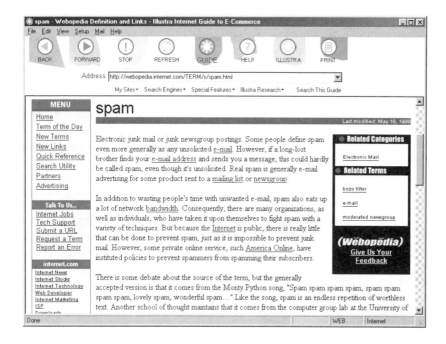

Many direct-marketing professionals view e-mail as manna from heaven, and list brokers have traded in e-mail addresses for many years. As with a lot of tactics such as these, most people only use them because they are successful, and there are plenty of Web sites that explain how they work, and how to integrate e-mail mailings with other marketing tools. You need to know about them, both because you will receive them and because you may want to send them as part of your business.

Is free e-mail worth it?

The number of people with e-mail has escalated sharply in the past year or so, thanks to free e-mail services such as Hotmail. These are usually accessed through a Web page and make it possible to get and send messages anywhere that you can log on to the Net. The phenomenal growth of cybercafés in such traveller-friendly destinations as Thailand and Australia is testament to how convenient such services can be when you're on the move.

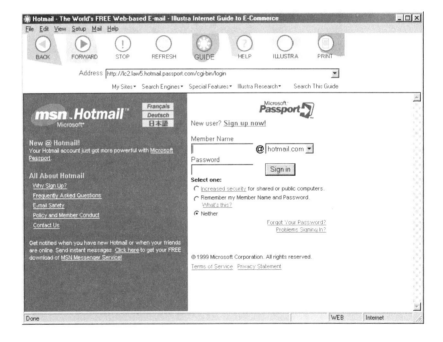

While free systems are great for personal use, most business people will be looking for something slightly different, both in terms of security and the desire to link e-mail in with their overall online presence. There is little credibility in using a Hotmail account for business, compared to owning a domain name (eg, www.yourbusinessname.co.uk) and having an e-mail address to go with it.

Many-to-many e-mail

This type of e-mail communication is becoming recognized by many in the Net-literate business community as an important part of building lasting relationships with customers. You can send customized e-mails to them and they can e-mail you and each other to take part in online discussions. You can use a free service (such as eGroups) or you can buy software to build this capability into your Web site.

Newsgroups

Newsgroups are considered a nether region of the Internet, not usually travelled by the average Internet punter and populated by mythological Internet gurus who swap hackers' codes, dirty pictures and inane gossip. This is all true, but there is more to it than that.

Somewhere in your e-mail package or Web browser you'll have 'stumbled across' something to do with newsgroups, or read about them in magazines or an Internet guidebook. It is very easy to ignore them as it requires a bit of work to get the best out of them, but you may find pearls of wisdom, new contacts or the answer to a technical question, which makes it all worthwhile.

This is not news

The first point is that newsgroups are not full of news. They are electronic forums that discuss specific topics, identified by a name such as uk.jobs.wanted, alt.biz.misc, or even alt.recovery.cow-fetish. Anyone can post a message to a forum, and everyone subscribed to it will receive it. Everyone else in the group can then see any reply to the message.

At its simplest a newsgroup is a straightforward discussion tool, enabling people with similar interests to ask questions, share information and swap gossip. There may be a group relating to the trade you're in, a country you're interested in exporting to, or a piece of software you're having problems with. It may be a useful source of advice, a way of raising your profile in a niche market, or somewhere to check out your ideas before presenting them to your boss.

There are some 25,000 of those groups out there, running through a piece of technology called Usenet. The whole thing is e-mail based, and to join the discussion you need to be subscribed to a group. Netscape's and Microsoft's browser packages include software for reading newsgroups, but it does take a bit of setting up for the beginner.

Another route into the world of newsgroups is the amazing www.deja.com. This site catalogues the messages on nearly every newsgroup, and has archives going back to 1995 on some lists. It has a search facility to help track down useful groups, and lots of other add-ons to link you into related stuff. It has recently become more of a portal to consumers, but you can still find what you want from newsgroups if you 'dig deep'.

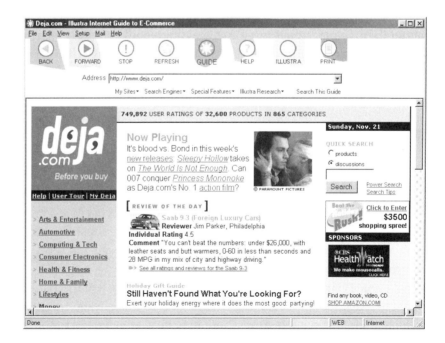

Using newsgroups

Newsgroups are not for everyone. They can seem difficult to use and often appear to be inhabited by people who are either too knowledgeable or simply too intimidating to deal with. But they could be a great source of help and many people swear by them for up-to-the minute interaction with others anywhere in the world.

Specialist newsreader software is available to help make reading easy and you can download messages when you check your e-mail. They can be delivered amongst your regular e-mail, or browsed online. You can keep tabs on any number of lists by using the software to subscribe to them, and either check them as they come in or leave half an hour aside now and then to read back through recent messages.

To find the best list for you, go to www.deja.com and start searching for subjects. Many newsgroups relate to recreational activity, so serious business information can be hard to come by at first. Have a good 'rummage around' the site, though, use the search facilities, think laterally, join lists you like the look of, and you'll soon get the hang of it.

Newsgroups are not the most user-friendly of technologies and there's no point spending frustrated hours trying to make them work for you. But they're obviously only there because they work for millions of people, and it's just possible they could work for you.

5

Marketing and the Internet

Introduction

For ease of use, the Top 200 Web sites for marketing are arranged by topic. This section offers a brief overview of each. For fast access to the sites mentioned here, install the CD ROM on your PC and click directly on their names (this way you won't have to type Web site addresses into your Internet browser).

In this section we give you an idea of what you can expect to find within each topic and what the Web sites can offer. Remember that the Web is constantly changing, so make sure you update your guide regularly by visiting the Illustra Web site. You can do this by clicking on the Illustra button once your guide is installed on your PC.

General resources

Making the most of the Internet is often about knowing cheaper, quicker or more convenient ways of doing something online than you could offline. It is also about being selective over which sites you visit and what you do when you get there. Many useful snippets of information can be 'dug up' if you start 'digging' in the right place. More and more services are being developed to make this information more accessible.

Whatever business you're in, there are some useful general sites for the marketing practitioner. These offer a good starting point if you're new online, and may offer something of particular interest on an ongoing basis. The **American Express Small Business Exchange**, for example, is a suite of sites that includes general information, more specialist advice and links to useful information elsewhere.

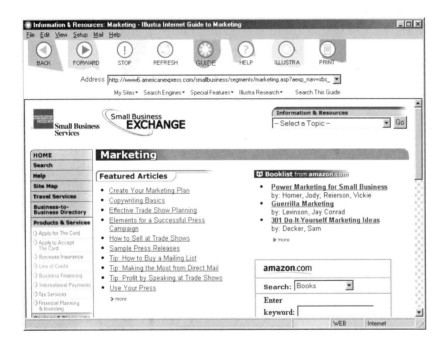

DIY marketing advice

All marketing professionals are aware that they would benefit from knowing which strategies and tactics really work and which don't. This is why many Web sites offer case studies, news and tips, giving users a taste of what other people are doing and how it's working.

Many offer regular e-mail newsletters giving more examples, and, of course, many of these examples benefit from any specialist service the host site provides.

The soft-sell approach doesn't mean the information is worthless, however, and there is plenty of valuable advice available for free. Much of it covers marketing on the Internet, but there's also advice about drawing up business plans and tips relevant to every business.

'Avoid wearing patterned clothing, especially on the upper half of the body, because it will shorten the attention span of the person with whom you are speaking.' This was found on the **Marketing Magic** site, which is maintained by a marketing company and avoids the hard sell to offer sensible advice on a range of issues (almost all of it more useful than the above comment).

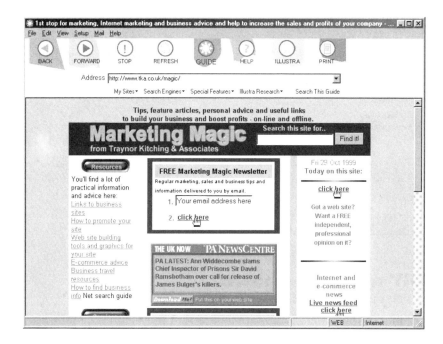

On the other hand, **Marketing UK** covers a range of information, has few apparent links with commercial services, and provides a range of useful information that you can easily print out to read at your own convenience.

Many sites such as this also have a free e-mail newsletter. In the e-mail lists section of the guide you'll find sites that collect a range of newsletters. Check them out and choose the best you've found if you want to subscribe to a newsletter but don't want your e-mail inbox filling up with messages you haven't got time to read.

Trade and professional organizations

The sites of trade associations and professional organizations can provide useful background information and checking them out can help the first-time Internet user. They are generally in the 'dull but worthy' category described in Chapter 3. The good ones offer services to users rather than simply reproducing brochures and offering contact phone numbers. They make you realize how bad the poor sites are. The best examples can help the professional work better, usually through a combination of services run on the site and the range of links they offer.

There is a growing range of educational material online, although very little is published by UK-based professional organizations. The **Direct Marketing Association** has a very useful site if you want to attend its courses, but **www.marketfiles.net** offers basic case studies as part of its business of selling fuller reports – and registration is free.

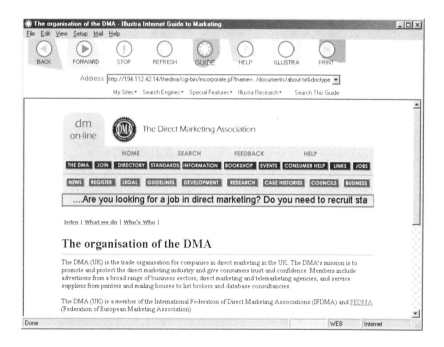

For heavyweight academic consideration of the latest marketing issues, especially as they relate to the Internet, check out a site like

Net Academy on Business Media, which is part of the Swiss-based Net Academy.

Advertising

Key points

- The Internet has some useful reference information about the UK advertising industry.
- You can learn as much as you like about the art of advertising online, but most of the information has a US flavour.
- Business to business services are limited, but growing fast.
- You will find lots of very sophisticated sites that are barely disguised 'corporate brochures'.

As you may expect from the advertising industry, there are numerous very good-looking sites out there, especially from the big agencies around the world. However, perhaps unsurprisingly, most do little more than provide the creative team with somewhere to play with their new technology gizmo and explain at great length how wonderful their agency is.

Of course, if you're looking for an agency, this is good news, as you can browse its portfolio, link through to its clients' sites and find out more. But if you're looking for useful information to help plan an advertising campaign it is unlikely that you'll want to trawl through many 'flashy Flash' sites.

So what about something practical like selecting an agency? This often starts with a bit of desk research. Those 'corporate brochures' can be useful for seeing what an agency is doing, and it may be worth putting an agency's name into a search engine and seeing what you find. The popular search engines are easily accessible in the guide – click on Search Engines in the Fast Find Menu Bar. It is slightly easier to use the **Institute of Practitioners of Advertising** searchable members list as a starting point than a general search engine. You can find this in Advertising – Organizations or by using the Search This Guide feature.

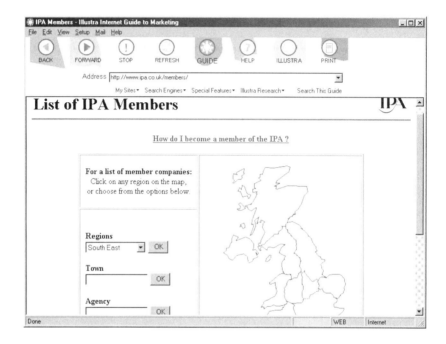

News about what's happening in the world of advertising can also offer pointers to agencies and creative work being planned. Knowing what's coming along, who's doing what and, most importantly, what works, is a very basic part of the intelligence gathering most marketing people need. Advertising tactics can make or break any campaign and 'keeping your nose to the ground' can make decision-making much easier.

News and information about advertising is offered by sites such as **mad.co.uk**. This is an aggregation of 13 marketing-related titles published by Centaur, including *Precision Marketing, Marketing Week* and *Creative Review*. The registration process is a bit 'in your face', but the site provides a great way of drawing on the combined content of several titles, to offer a new kind of service. Other media titles are also moving their news online, but mad.co.uk is a particularly good example.

If you're interested in online advertising there's an almost unlimited number of sites to visit, each promising you more eyeballs, giving higher CTRs (Click Through Rates) and delivering more JPS (Jargon Per Sentence) than the next. Many focus almost exclusively on the US market and, whilst the global marketplace is inching ever closer, this can be annoying.

Channel Seven is one of many similar sites that offer a slightly broader view of online advertising. For more detailed news about the UK online industry and its use of advertising, have a look at **New Media Age**.

Finding an agency is all very well if you can afford one, but what about buying your own space? There is a wealth of information available online about various UK media, often listed on the help-fully titled **Media UK**. This site carries listings of different media, offers statistics about coverage, and is a good basic guide for the beginner.

Some commercial services endear themselves to their public by going the extra mile and hosting useful information. With all its talk of brand loyalty, this is something you might expect the adver-tising industry to excel at. **Adweb**, for example, offers Web site design and hosting services, but also maintains a helpful reference source on UK and international media, advertising and marketing. Lists such as these provide a much better jumping-off point than a list of search engine results, but few purely commercial sites offer something this productive and as likely to keep the average punter coming back for more.

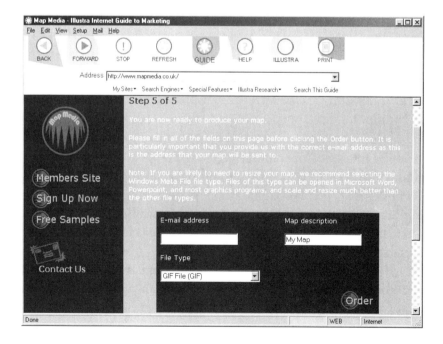

A little further along the learning curve is a service from **Map Media**, which enables you to input a postcode and receive details of the media covering that area. The site allows you to request a sample map free of charge before you decide whether you want to pay for one. Similar online business to business services are likely to emerge in the next phase of the Internet revolution, but for the time being this is one of the disappointingly few sites to embrace online transactions.

Finally, it's worth considering whether these offerings can deliver to their advertisers the audiences they claim. The **Audit Bureau of Circulations** monitors readership information across a range of print titles in the UK and is considering how to do the same for online advertising media. It's quite a challenge, but the site explains something of how it is going about it, as well as offering paid-for access to data from its systems.

6

Direct marketing and international marketing

Direct marketing long predates the Internet, but with the advent of electronic communications addressed to individual customers, a major transformation is taking place. The Internet makes it easier for small companies to think about marketing internationally, and there are plenty of tools available to help.

This chapter shows you how the guide can help you use the Internet more effectively to research in this area. Remember, though, it'll be much quicker, easier and more comprehensive if you install the CD ROM on your PC.

Direct marketing

Key points

- The Internet is a new direct-marketing medium containing lots of information about how to use e-mail effectively.

- There are some online services offering lists for sale.

- Helpful news and information is available for the direct marketing professional.

The flexibility, economy and sheer power of database technology has given a 'shot in the arm' to direct marketing in recent years. The expansion of the Internet as a consumer and business environment has given added impetus to this growth, and the use of e-mail as a marketing weapon is transforming traditional relationships into the one-to-one precision marketing of the future.

The **Royal Mail** naturally takes a keen interest in helping direct marketers make better use of postal-based activities. Its Web site is full of information to help get the most from mailings, whether through a simple postage calculator, links to international services or access to its lists services. And you can buy stamps online, too.

The Internet can provide direct access to valuable data for direct mail and telemarketing campaigns, information for planning and controlling sales campaigns and the ability to download lists directly into your own PC. **Yellow Pages** offers direct marketing services, especially list buying, through its Business Database site. This is a paid-for service, but offers direct access to lists that can be downloaded or supplied on disk.

Dun and Bradstreet have a similar service on their site. The search facility draws upon their database of 1.6 million UK businesses, providing search options across a range of parameters through the Web page. Just click on a few boxes to tell it who you're targeting – sector, location, size, etc – and it will perform a count. Sample data can be downloaded for free as labels or plain text, and buying online is straightforward once you've decided it meets your requirements.

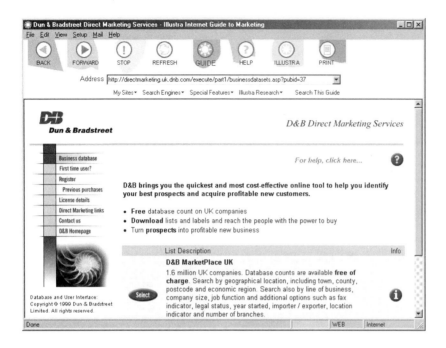

Both **Yellow Pages** and **Dun and Bradstreet** are great examples of the business to business services that are sure to become more commonplace as the Internet becomes an everyday part of the business environment. Other services exist but these two will provide what you need now.

The Web offers a lot of information about how to exploit the Internet as a direct marketing medium, but it is absurdly difficult to avoid information about pyramid selling and multi-level marketing.

For a first step see Direct marketing – E-mail marketing, for a simple guide to adding e-mail to your marketing arsenal. The **1-to-1 Web Site** from Process Request specializes in building and fulfilling sales and marketing relationships through e-mail, and a free print guide can be ordered from the site. It arrives promptly and is excellent background reading to set the creative juices flowing. This is not to endorse their services, but to point out that it does provide an excellent example of how to use the Internet to introduce yourself to new potential customers.

It is certain that e-mail will grow and grow as a direct marketing medium, despite concerns about 'spam' (unsolicited bulk e-mail) and confidentiality. Web sites such as **dmnews.com**, and **Precision Marketing** offer a way of keeping tabs on developments.

Anyone in the direct marketing business needs to start thinking about how to integrate e-mail into their campaigns; this is also a great medium for seeing what others are doing, as well as a way of keeping track of what is possible. Visit the Web sites of competitors, specialist news sites and trade associations as regularly as you would thumb through any trade magazine, and join e-mail lists that offer news delivered to your in-tray. See what everyone else is doing and work out how it can deliver results for you.

Real people, available now

Data can be downloaded direct from the Internet through various business to business services, as list management services have well and truly embraced the online era. You can carry out free research for prospective campaigns by trawling the stores of information held by big names such as **Yellow Pages** and **Dun and Bradstreet** and buy lists online to be sent straight to your desktop. Get online now to find information you can use for:

- direct mail;
- telemarketing campaigns;
- sales campaign planning and control;
- new product or service launches;
- market or sector analysis.

International marketing

Key points

- Find global information at your fingertips.
- Access background information, up-to-date news and market intelligence.
- Take advantage of useful business services online.

Most people developing markets outside their existing domestic boundaries think of using Web sites to attract and inform new customers. The guide's International Marketing section shows that the Internet offers an enormous resource for desktop research, which underpins any successful marketing activity. You can find out more about new markets, research prospective clients, keep up to date with local news, access government support through trade shows, and download statistical data for analysis.

The global nature of the Internet promises to blur international boundaries, and some pundits predict that we will eventually be operating in one single global marketplace. Of course people are always going to shop, work and have fun in their own backyard, but the ability to deliver the same service to any part of the planet through the Internet means international e-commerce is now fact, not advertising fiction. This is true of both consumer and business to business markets, whether dealing in products or services.

For instant international news the **CNNfn** site matches the TV service for its ability to deliver global news across sectors, as does **ft.com** from the *Financial Times*. Both provide a host of services alongside the basic news facility, but the FT's country reports and easily searched archives of news make it an essential point of contact on a regular basis.

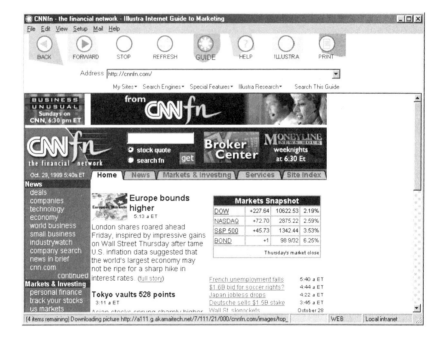

The government's **Foreign and Commonwealth Office** site is full of excellent up-to-date information about trade and travel abroad. An e-mail service can keep you informed of developments, and the site has links to many other government sites covering trade initiatives, and other business-oriented information. It also has a neat facility to enable you to customize the page to meet your particular interests.

Read all about what's really happening

It's a struggle to keep up with events in another country through the meagre international news coverage in UK media titles, but online there's a feast of information being published in the country of origin. Whether it's trade or travel information, up-to-date political news, or contact with business partners, the Internet brings the whole world closer, through Web pages and e-mail.

If you have business in a specific country you probably have contacts who can point you at useful Web sites, so get their e-mail address and start swapping tips. Otherwise try looking for news and media titles with Web pages by searching through lists such as **Kidon Media Link**. It's not pretty but it does seem to contain links to more online publications than you can shake a stick at.

If you have trouble reading foreign language stories then services such as **Babelfish** offer very basic facilities for translating live online. Or contact someone who can pop pop for you and get them to deliver relevant news straight to your in-tray using e-mail. Commercial online translation services offer flexible services and quick turnaround times, which can also be helpful for sorting out business documents. Or find a foreign-language speaker at your end and give them Internet access in return for market intelligence.

Making the best use of what's available online is down to some basic information-gathering skills and regular practice. In international research this puts a lot of the burden on the marketing person to sift, analyse and interpret information, whilst 'digging for the nuggets' that are worth returning to again and again.

To get an idea of how to carry out research online, try a simple guide from a commercial service like **RBA Information Services**. RBA offer training in how to use the Internet as a research tool, and this is a valuable jumping-off point if you're going to get the most from international marketing resources. You may even want to pay them to teach you since skills such as these will become an ever more powerful weapon in the marketer's armoury.

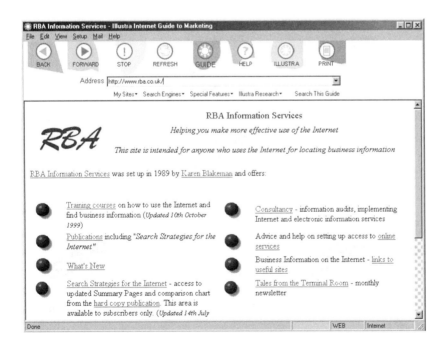

British Trade International, one of a number of excellent British government sites, offers basic country reports, tips for first time exporters, useful telephone numbers, e-mail contacts and more. This is a great place to start since it offers leads into other sites relevant to the exporter, plus news of events, licence information and so on.

The **Institute of Export** also provides a useful stopping-off point, with news, contacts and advice.

Travel goodies: those useful little extras

Like a foldable toothbrush and your battered bedside alarm-torch-radio-Teasmade-trouser-press, there are some things you just can't do without when travelling the world's trade routes. Check details of your destination before you go by using the **British Airways mini-guides**.

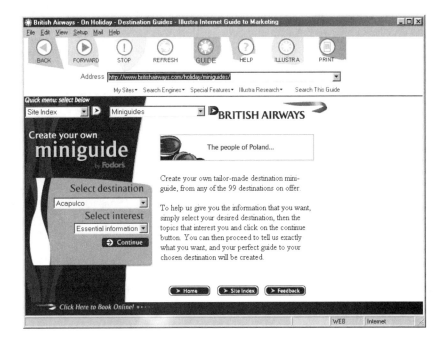

Or use **multimap.com** for a map of just about anywhere.

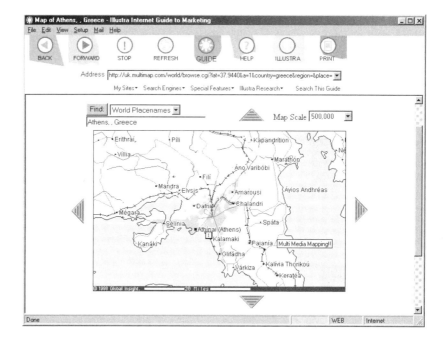

A2B Travel offers ticket bookings, travel information, weather checks, flight arrivals and will even sell you a book to while away the flight (see Business essentials).

The European Union

A final mention for Europe and the single market, for which the selection of Web sites has to be one of the most mind-bogglingly boring on the planet. Very few official EU sites offer much to the average business user, preferring to home in on the needs of the committed bureaucrat, with text heavy, jargon-riddled, impenetrably dense pages about rules and regulations.

Some sites do focus on trade opportunities, such as the FCO site mentioned above, and the helpful and easy to use **Euro Info Centre** (see International Marketing – Europe).

There is also a fair bit about the impact of the euro, with the British Government pitching in with its **Get Ready for the Euro** site. This turns out to be mostly uninspiring, however, with little of practical use on offer.

7

Internet marketing

Key points

- There are lots of sites about how to do it.
- There are lots of examples to learn from.
- You'll find free tools and services to do it yourself.
- Start with basic marketing principles to get the most from putting your business online.

Any serious marketing professional must by now have picked up on the Internet revolution and be starting to investigate the online opportunities. Despite the near hysterical hype about e-commerce changing our lives, it's clear that the rise of the Net is altering some of the basic assumptions of business practice.

In marketing, the shift may well be easier to deal with; assuming that a marketing-focused organization is already adapted to the needs of its customers the Internet represents an opportunity to reach more people in new ways. But where does it fit in the marketing mix?

The Internet can be seen as a promotional medium, a means of distributing products and services (eg online banking) and a cost-effective medium for selling products. It offers benefits in business to business and consumer markets and can help reach untapped pockets of local and regional markets, as well as putting a business on the global marketing map. It is an extension of existing uses of new technology in the marketing toolbox, sitting alongside databases, spreadsheets and mail merges, but is also a powerful new source of information, intelligence and direct relationships with customers, suppliers and others.

The best way to see how to use the Internet as a promotional medium is to use the guide to go online and look for specific products, cheaper suppliers or your main competitors. As with any medium, when investigating Web sites you need to develop your ability to spot certain types of presentation and to see through the promotional fluff to the true value of what's on offer. You also need to understand how closely Web-based advertising can be integrated with other aspects of a campaign. The introduction to Web site types in Chapter 3 helps build a vocabulary that highlights key characteristics and provides a shorthand to recognize sites that will become increasingly sophisticated as familiarity grows.

When it comes to marketing your product online, the Americans got there first. In particular, a random search for 'marketing' in a search engine is likely to lead to the frenzied world of the multi-level marketers (MLM) or pyramid sellers. This medium is perfect for building connections and networks but there are all sorts of scams and tactics in use. It may be of interest to see how the new medium can be used, but note that the marketing tactics are as different on the Internet as they are in everyday life.

It is useful to try to keep track of key developments and their successes and failures in building markets online. Two obvious examples to look at are **Amazon.com** and **egg.com**. For different reasons they represent a whole new way of building brand awareness, offering new products and delivering through new channels. They have had to develop a new infrastructure for their services and market themselves to consumers in new ways.

They both seem highly successful, achieving an astonishing rate of awareness amongst key audiences in next to no time.

Amazon.com has an extensive network of affiliates selling its books from Web sites around the globe – a completely new type of marketing relationship but built on old-fashioned principles – whilst egg.com uses TV advertising to help differentiate itself from existing banking products.

Follow their progress through marketing magazines to understand how they are achieving such high-profile success, or check out news sites such as **Revolution**, a Haymarket print title with an excellent Web site (see Internet marketing – Resources).

Despite its US bias, a searchable site such as **ChannelSeven.com** is also worth 'trawling' for snippets, inspiration and background detail.

To get going with your Internet marketing you'll need to get to know your potential audience. In a business-to-business environment you may already be swapping e-mails and checking

Web pages with clients, suppliers and others. But are you using it to find out who else is out there? Have a look at **Nua Surveys** for detailed reports on who's already online plus thoughts about who will be soon. Nua is an Irish site that collects and disseminates information for free.

A regular slice of wisdom is a helpful thing when dealing with new ideas. Many sites have built their identity around the views of a guru-like commentator, who proffers opinions on his or her particular subject via e-mail to an expectant worldwide audience. Well almost. Some of these sites are obviously more useful than others, so see what you get out of one, but don't be afraid to go looking for another. They will usually offer daily, weekly or monthly versions of their online insight so be sure to choose one that fits with your ability to read long e-mails.

An example worth checking out is Jim Sterne's site called **Target Marketing**. His column draws upon years of marketing online and his books are straightforward and written with the marketing profession in mind, rather than revelling in the technology.

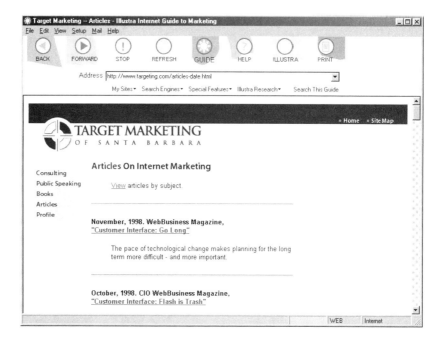

As well as news bulletins from the main magazines, someone like Gerry McGovern at **Nua Surveys** will post you a regular column giving his views on online business. This is usually witty, easily digested and generally thought provoking.

Sell yourself online

What could be easier than Internet marketing? Get online and do the research; develop an Internet marketing strategy; recruit an agency and build a Web site. Incorporate all sorts of interactive features, online transactions and useful extras. Sit back and wait for the visitor statistics to rack up and the money to start rolling in. Er. . . maybe.

Once you're active online there are lots of ways of keeping people coming to your site, but doing nothing definitely isn't one of them. A good Web design/marketing agency will register you with search engines, keep an eye on the keywords used on your site and make sure it is up to date. It's possible to assess which parts of your site receive the most visits, and to adjust your tactics accordingly, as well as to look at where your visitors came from, to decide whether advertising campaigns are working.

Trying to capture data about visitors is difficult, and online forms are frequently either overlooked or abused. Registration systems help you see who's coming, but they put a lot of people off if they don't come with specific benefits that make it worth completing the form. And it has to be really valuable to persuade people not to lie about themselves, so don't rely on them. Use registration forms, but don't forget to offer subscription to an e-mail mailing list (and make sure it complies with the Data Protection Act to be sure you can use it).

Your online marketing campaign can increase traffic to your site, but are you converting your advertising spend into sales? Keep track of those sales attributed in some way to your online activity, and log the statistics for your site from day one to keep track of how things are going. Build new relationships with owners of other sites to increase the number of visitors with a specific interest – rather like a referral system. Affiliate schemes, such as those run by Amazon, reward you for people linking into their site, so consider them as a possible source of revenue and to add functionality to your site.

Spend time online yourself, looking at where else your visitors have been, checking their Web pages and getting a feel for the niche that you inhabit. Answer e-mail enquiries as promptly as you would phone calls or postal enquiries, and make sure your Web site address appears on every single piece of printed material you produce.

There is more to marketing online than building a Web site and putting the address on your headed paper. As the medium matures it will be increasingly important to understand its capabilities and how to integrate them with other tactics. To build an online strategy for your business try looking at the one of the UK marketing information sites, such as **Marketing UK** (introduced in Chapter 5) or for business-to-business markets look at **Net Marketing**. These sites offer basic information with a marketing slant to help start your thinking or refresh your ideas.

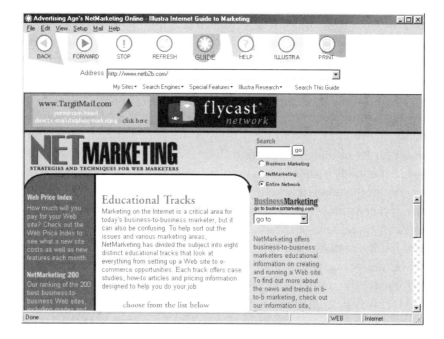

It becomes clear quite quickly that whilst the mechanics of the relationship may be different, and the possibilities for developing new markets may be greater, a lot of Internet marketing is delivered through old-fashioned marketing sweat. It's about being clear about your audience and how to reach them efficiently, understanding people's needs, offering products or services to meet them and delivering in a way that they want.

Spending on advertising online is rising fast, and many Web sites already subsist solely on income from advertisers. As with traditional media choices this is an area that needs careful research before splashing hundreds or thousands of pounds on a campaign.

There are plenty of people out there willing to offer advice, so it needn't take long to get to grips with the jargon and the possible benefits of using banners, sponsorship, affiliate schemes and so on. However, as with a lot of the newest developments in online business, UK resources are very thin on the ground and it may be useful to join a few mailing lists to get a feel for the sites people recommend.

A good starting point for online media news and views is the UK Net Marketing list, which can be joined at **chinwag**. This is like walking invisibly into a room of experts, being able to hear what everyone's talking about and having the chance to ask questions whenever you need, either in public or just one to one.

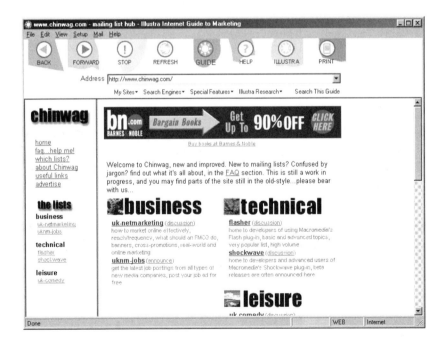

If you're not happy with the messages you receive each day, you may want to look for more appropriate lists through **Mouse Tracks**, a list of marketing-related mailing lists.

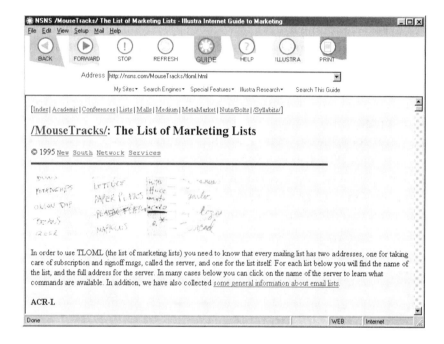

Don't forget to keep your ear to the ground for lists recommended by people in your trade, or other marketing people. You may find yourself discussing key issues in public spaces, some of which have searchable archives, so be cautious about revealing details of your next big campaign or gossiping about your boss. But mailing lists can encourage a healthy flow of information and can open the door to co-operation – the next wave of business-to-business relationships that could see you benefit from teaming up with a former rival.

8

Marketing news and events

News and magazines

Key points

- There is lots of news available on lots of subjects.
- It's not always easy to find specialist resources but mainstream information can be a useful starting point.
- Many sites offer a useful e-mail service.

The Internet is alive with news and current affairs information on every subject under the sun, including marketing. All the major UK broadsheets are there, as are most international titles and the large dailies in most countries, plus specialist magazines, new titles and Internet-only sources of news. Finding news on any subject is possible, but remember, just because you know it's there doesn't mean you'll find it.

The **BBC Business News** Web site (see News and magazines – Business news) is a good place to start when checking out news. It has many different sections including a mainstream business news service with an international flavour that may be enough for the average businessperson to keep tabs on the news.

For more detailed information the *Financial Times* site **ft.com** should be top of most people's list. It has transferred its authoritative coverage to the Internet, but has also added a host of features that begin to develop the true potential of online news resources. Its search facilities are amongst the most comprehensive available and it makes use of archives from a wide range of titles. It is necessary to register to access many of the add-on services, but most are free. There is a charge for accessing certain items in the archive, such as specialist reports, but most are cheap (a few pounds) and could be exactly what you're looking for. As with many Web sites, it is useful to spend time burrowing in the nooks and crannies. For example, the *Financial Times* site includes discussion forums usually involving issues related to IT, but at the time of review it included questions about the value of Internet stocks.

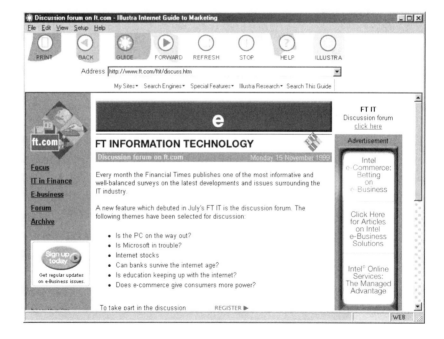

The ability to provide a basis for two-way interaction helps promote a site's role within a sector, as well as generating more for visitors to see on a casual browse.

Delivering news by e-mail is now a common way of maintaining links with readers. Many news and magazine sites use it to highlight new stories as they appear online, whilst others deliver whole stories within an e-mail, usually with links through to the Web page to encourage further reading. Whatever approach they use, this is an excellent service for the regular e-mail user and especially for those who pay for their Web access. Reading stories whilst offline is considerably cheaper than trawling through a Web site for them.

The news that comes to you

There are many, many sites that will send you e-mail at the drop of a hat, but deciding which ones are useful is best done through trial and error. It's usually simple to subscribe, and there's no need to be too honest if you're worried about getting junk mail. You may also want to set up a free e-mail address specifically for subscriptions.

News and opinion about online marketing are very popular, with everyone keen to pass judgement on the best way of making money on the Internet. Jesse Berst's Anchordesk feature for **ZDNet** is a good example of regular, US-based Internet-related news, which is often not featured in the UK press but is valuable for people keeping their eye on developments.

Several marketing sites listed in this guide will send news and updates and, with some glaring exceptions, will generally not try to be 'cunningly concealed commercials'. The **Press Association** will deliver a daily briefing of the top stories, linked through to its site, and you can get an often wry view of commercial change from Gerry McGovern, a writer for the Irish **Nua Surveys**.

Stopping the messages should be no more difficult than sending an e-mail to an automated mailing list telling it to stop, so if your in-tray starts filling up at an alarming rate you can easily stem the tide.

Events and conferences

Key point

The Internet provides advance notice of exhibitions, conferences and other events. Many Web sites provide industry news and information for the UK marketing trade, and magazines such as *Campaign* and *Marketing Week* have Web sites that provide advance notices, reviews and other helpful information. There are also specialist sites that host data on forthcoming shows, often on a global basis.

The American Express **Small Business Exchange** site has an extensive list of events, for example. It's easy to search and although information is mostly US-based it's easy to add details of your own events and provides links to other useful resources elsewhere on the Net. The **Amex** site also includes helpful background information and news for business people in a number of sectors, some of which is specifically produced for a UK audience.

Closer to home are Web sites such as **the biz**, which also has a searchable list of trade shows and sector-specific events with links through to relevant Web pages.

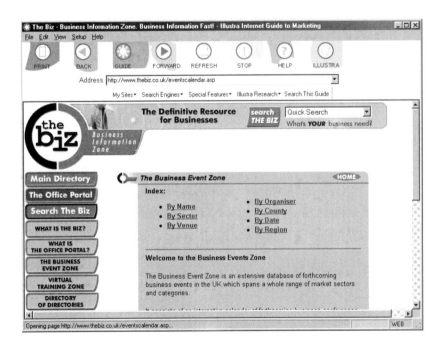

The **Trade Fairs and Exhibitions UK** site does what it says on the box, whilst the **Advertising Association** holds details of events of particular interest to UK-based marketing professionals.

Flying high

The senior executive who jets between conferences and seminars across the globe should check out **The Economist Conferences** for details of forthcoming events.

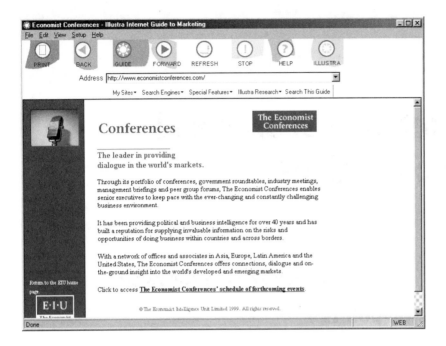

Conferences

The Economist Conferences

The leader in providing
dialogue in the world's markets.

Through its portfolio of conferences, government roundtables, industry meetings, management briefings and peer group forums, The Economist Conferences enables senior executives to keep pace with the ever-changing and constantly challenging business environment.

It has been providing political and business intelligence for over 40 years and has built a reputation for supplying invaluable information on the risks and opportunities of doing business within countries and across borders.

With a network of offices and associates in Asia, Europe, Latin America and the United States, The Economist Conferences offers connections, dialogue and on-the-ground insight into the world's developed and emerging markets.

Click to access **The Economist Conferences' schedule of forthcoming events**.

© The Economist Intelligence Unit Limited 1999. All rights reserved.

9

Marketing research and public relations

Marketing research

Key points

- Free information is available, but it's not always useful.
- There is lots of US information online.
- Commercial services offer online downloading of paid-for data straight to your desktop.

All good marketing relies upon research. Building banks of information about markets, competition, potential customers and spending habits is a vital part of good planning. Every marketing textbook describes the role of marketing research as part of the marketing plan, and will suggest what to look for, whether it's political, economic, social or technological change.

A key part of an efficient marketing research process lies in marketing intelligence, or the ability to gather useful information and data continuously from a variety of sources. A good marketing information system is the bedrock of larger intelligence systems, creating a structured approach to the gathering and dissemination of every 'nugget'. This may be beyond the reach of smaller companies, but most good marketers always have their antennae tuned to potential opportunities and have a good mental filing system allowing them to retrieve relevant information whenever necessary.

For any marketer, part of the attraction of being on the Internet is the ability to 'stumble across' information that fits into his or her planning awareness. Marketers can visit competitors' Web sites regularly to see what they're up to, join announcements e-mail lists to keep track of their tactics, search for information on them by trawling company listings services, and keep track of industry news through specialist online magazine sites. All these tactics may tell as much about them as can be learnt by any other means. Having a feel for what they're up to can be critical to decisions about marketing tactics, whether it's pricing, promotional campaigns or PR.

There is a lot of basic data available on the Internet, much of it fairly easy to access, free, and surprisingly up to date. The big research agencies are well represented, and some offer tasters from recent reports that cost thousands of pounds to buy. Whether or not you subsequently buy such reports, this is a good way to see what they could offer your business. Some of the executive summaries provide basic answers, so you may not need the detailed data available in the full report. **Durlacher, Dun and Bradstreet** and the **Economic Intelligence Unit** are amongst those publishing and selling research data online.

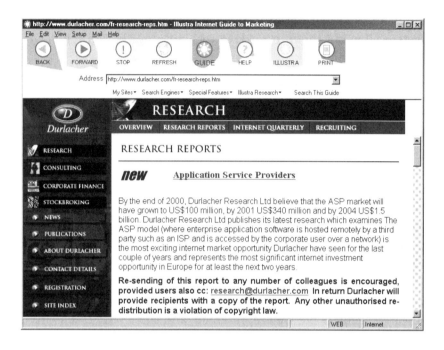

Media data for the UK can be found on several sites that offer relatively recent information about viewers, readers and listeners in various forms. Any publication using ABC to audit its circulation can be found at **Audit Bureau of Circulations**, for example, or check out **The UK National Readership Survey**. Magazines such as **Campaign**, **Media Week** and **Marketing** offer insights into which tactics work, and can also be found online.

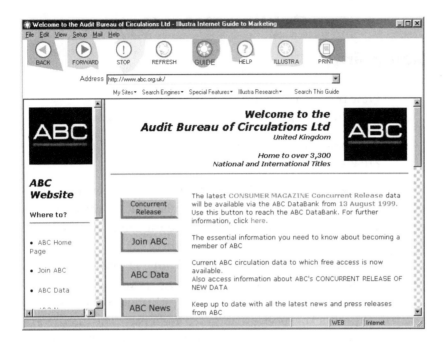

If you're starting to get serious about using Internet marketing it's worth joining mailing lists and subscribing to a few of the many e-mail services that deliver marketing insight direct to your mailbox. These will often be great sources of further information, so it can be worth a weekly scan to keep track on trends in a dynamic environment.

Getting the most out of researching online requires more than just knowing the address for Yahoo!. Visiting some of the sites mentioned in this guide will provide a springboard to information of specific interest to you. It's also worth checking out resources such as the How To guide produced by Karen Blakeman at **RBA Information Services**.

Public relations

Key points

- New press contacts are available online.
- Specialist news can be monitored through Web sites.
- Specialist services are most developed in the IT sector, but are growing across all press activity.

PR and marketing are regarded by many as entirely separate businesses but the boundaries are blurred. Whilst many of the tactics are different, several of the basic principles are the same, especially the need to start by thinking about your audience.

PR consultants, press officers and others in PR-related roles earn their money by keeping track of trends, spotting opportunities for press coverage and maintaining a steady flow of information about their product or service to targeted audiences. The Internet is a new medium for achieving this, and it is important that anyone responsible for a company's image is able to understand and use the Net to promote and raise awareness.

As with any new medium the rules of engagement have yet to be established, but in this case e-mail provides one of the most obvious starting points. Many journalists will be regular users of e-mail and are likely to prefer press release information to be delivered electronically, because they can cut and paste text into their work. But this doesn't mean that they're any more willing to receive unsolicited e-mail than the rest of us. Blanket e-mailing thousands of journalists may be a five-minute task, but few of the busiest (and hence most useful) journalists will use materials sent this way and it may harm your chances in the future.

Any PR works by developing a contact and building a relationship that is mutually beneficial. You will probably supply basic information in a press release as usual and call your contact to see if he or she is interested. But then offer access to background material by putting it on a Web page, create samples of your photo library on the Web so that people can easily ask for what they need, give e-mail addresses of your in-house experts and keep in e-mail contact to supply further details.

Services such as **Prnet** act as an online point of contact between those looking for press coverage and those doing the writing. Journalists are given free access to a database of press releases, stored in various categories and available for instant download.

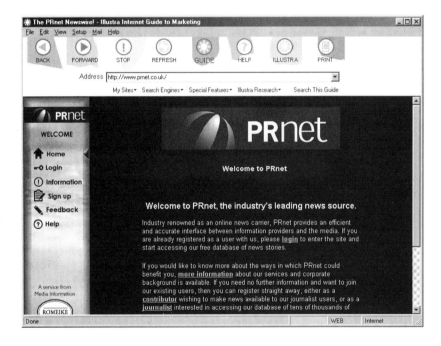

Stories appear here because press officers, PR agencies and others have subscribed to **PRnet**'s services and submitted stories. They pay for this as it has several benefits: journalists are actively seeking the stories through **PRnet** instead of ignoring the unsolicited press releases that can plague a busy hack's in-tray – and they reach journalists they might otherwise be unaware of; submitting one release is cheap; and there is an international dimension that most would not currently consider using. Not surprisingly this service seems to be most popular with the IT industry, but it is an example of an easy-to-use online service, useful for both parties involved, which will undoubtedly grow.

The Top 200 Web sites for marketing

Sub Topic	Title	Description	URL	Rele-vance	Ease of Use
BUSINESS ESSENTIALS					
BUSINESS INFORMATION		The following sites contain financial, company and product information of value to any business user.			
	Interactive Investor International	Register to get instant stock market quotes and access to some (occasionally) lively discussions from shareholders.	http://www.iii.co.uk/	1	3
	Yahoo! Finance UK & Ireland	Simple instant stock market quotes without registration.	finance.uk.yahoo.com/	1	4
	CAROL	A set of over 3000 company reports from large companies in the UK, Asia and Europe. Registration is free to companies, but coverage can be patchy. You are transferred to the company's Web site, so reports are not in a standard format.	www.carol.co.uk/	1	2
	Companies House	Model Web site, beautifully designed. You can search the database for company information but (strangely) only on Monday to Friday from 8 am to 8 pm.	www.companies-house.gov.uk	2	3

Sub Topic	Title	Description	URL	Rele-vance	Ease of Use
	How many online?	NUA Internet surveys collect data from around the world and give you the latest picture of how people have Internet access in different countries.	www.nua.ie/surveys/ how_many_online index.html	1	2
	UpMyStreet	Enter your postcode and find out what your neighbourhood's really like. Gives data on house prices, crime clear-up rates, schools, council tax, and, if you're feeling fragile, ambulance response times. More features promised soon.	www.upmystreet.com/	2	4
	Scoot	One of the most useful and friendly sites around. Search by business type and area for anything you need. Free registration is required to use the people finder, which claims 17 million names on its database.	www.scoot.co.uk/	4	5
TRAVEL		Getting about is so much easier with this kind of constantly updated information at your fingertips. These sites will provide a good excuse for spending money on a mobile Web terminal!			
	A2B Travel	A bit cluttered and not fully comprehensive, but this is the best general UK travel site we've encountered.	www.a2btravel.com/	3	2
	Expedia UK	Microsoft's UK travel site is an essential asset for the business traveller, but don't expect bargain travel here. It's simple to find scheduled flights, hotels and car hire in major cities and compare prices before you book.	expedia.co.uk/	3	4
	UK Public Transport Information	The site says 'If it's not here it's not on the Web' and for once it's not hype. Everything you need to know about public transport in any part of the UK.	www.pti.org.uk/	4	4

Sub Topic	Title	Description	URL	Rele- vance	Ease of Use
	Railtrack	If it's simply train times you want Railtrack's online timetable is the quickest way to get them. If would be even better if it prompted you for a return journey.	195.92.21.203/bin/ query.exe/en	4	3
	BAA Airport Information	Updates arrivals for major UK airports, plus a flight timetable. You can also find out what's in the shops to buy while you're waiting for the flight.	www.baa.co.uk/	4	4
	World maps	Not just any old maps but just about every kind of map that might be out there. Some are detailed enough to see the street you're headed for, but most provide political, economic or geographical information that may be useful if you don't know a country well.	www.lib.utexas.edu/ Libs/PCL/Map_ collection/Map_ collection.html	1	1
	OANDA Currency Converter	How many Albanian lek to the euro? No problem with this comprehensive and simple currency converter. You can also find historical rates for any day since 1990.	www.oanda.com/ converter/classic	3	4
	Multimap.com	A clickable map, down to street level, of the whole UK. Or simply enter a place name, or postcode, and you'll get a map that you can zoom in and out of. Terrific!	uk.multimap.com/ map/places.cgi	4	5
WEATHER AND TIME		Time to find out whether you need an umbrella.			
	The Met.Office	The weather – 'straight from the horse's mouth'.	www.meto.govt.uk/	1	4
	The World Clock	Is it too late to call Melbourne? Instant time anywhere in the world.	www.timeanddate. com/worldclock/	2	1
TELEPHONE AND POST		Essentials about essentials.			
	Postcodes On-line	Find addresses from postcodes and vice versa.	www.royalmail.co.uk/ paf/pcodefin.htm	4	4

Sub Topic	Title	Description	URL	Relevance	Ease of Use
	UK Telephone code locator	In which part of the country is that number beginning 01736? (Penzance, actually). What's the code for Penrith? A simple and handy tool developed by an enthusiast.	www.warwick.ac.uk/ cgi-bin-Phones/nng	2	1
	BT PhoneNet UK	The UK phone book online. Even if you pay a dial-up call, it's cheaper than dialling 192.	www.bt.com/ phonenetuk/	4	4
	BT Friends and Family	Change your friends and family numbers at a stroke. You can also check the current status of your phone bill.	www.customer-service. bt.com/friends_ family/owa/bestfriend. who	2	2
NEWS AND MEDIA		The best sites we've found for information about television, radio, newspapers and magazines.			
	BBC News	The front page of the BBC's news Web site. You can link directly to the last news bulletin on the World Service or on BBC1 television, if your browser's equipped for sound and video.	news.bbc.co.uk/	2	4
	AskMagpie	Links to over 7000 magazines and often very specialist journals organized by subject in a well-laid-out front page. Sounds daunting, but a simple search engine allows title and subject searches. Many have Web links, but if not there are fax and phone numbers.	www.askmagpie.com/	3	4
	Media UK Internet Directory	A really comprehensive index to media resources. The use of sound quickly becomes irritating, but you'll need it turned up for the live TV and radio. Aims to please all, but would benefit by organizing the resources according to who the user is.	www.mediauk.com/ directory/	3	3
	World Newspapers Online	Lovely interface with clickable map to reach 120+ English-language newspapers across the world.	www.alumni.adweb. co.uk/wno/	1	3

Sub Topic	Title	Description	URL	Rele-vance	Ease of Use
	Teletext	Millions of people regularly use this service on their TV – on your computer it looks much better and is much easier to use.	www1.teletext.co.uk/	2	1
	TVPlus	Quick and simple guide to what is on the five terrestrial TV channels in your region, plus a few satellite channels in peak time only.	www1.teletext.co.uk/ tv_new/	1	1
WRITING AIDS		The online aids can be really useful for report writing – especially if you have a permanent connection to the Internet.			
	thesaurus.com	A simple online *Roget's Thesaurus*. You can put in UK spellings but will be given US spellings.	www.thesaurus.com/	1	2
	dictionary.com	Simple online dictionary based on Webster's.	www.dictionary.com/	1	2
	OneLook Dictionaries	If you're really stuck or a true word lover you'll get hooked on this database, which claims to look at 2.8 million words in 566 dictionaries.	www.onelook.com/	1	2
	Webopedia	Look up what all that computer jargon means. If you really want to impress in 'techie' circles click on the recently added items and add them to your 'geekspeak'.	webopedia. internet.com/	2	3
	Whatis?com	Much more than a technical dictionary, this site has exploration sections on various topics, including how the Internet works, and speeds of connection. Try the learning paths section for excellent essay on technology-related topics such as 'convergence'.	www.whatis.com/	2	4

Sub Topic	Title	Description	URL	Rele-vance	Ease of Use
	infoplease.com	A huge US-based site with a huge number of … facts!	www.infoplease.com/	1	2
	Microsoft Encarta	Microsoft's cut-down free online version of Encarta might find out what you need, if you can bear the hard sell for the subscription version.	www.encarta. msn.com	1	2
LAW AND MONEY		General resources – often enough to tell you whether you need to pay for professional advice.			
	adviceguide	A service from the Citizens Advice Bureau – well designed and easy to use.	www.adviceguide. org.uk/nacab/plsql/ nacab.homepage	1	3
	buy.co.uk	A simple but hugely effective idea. Put in your postcode and latest bill and you can see whether you'll save money by switching electricity or gas suppliers. Compares mobile phone tariffs as well.	www.buy.co.uk/	3	4
FOR ADVANCED USERS		These are free resources for those seriously into the Internet, or who work all day on a keyboard.			
	EBoz!	Links and tips for anyone involved in building or running a Web site, or who'd like to. Expert advice, case studies and discussion forums, and plenty of free downloads to get you going.	www.eboz.com/ index.shtml	1	4
	AnyDay.com	If you use an electronic organizer or a program such as Microsoft Outlook you'll find this a terrific idea. You can store your information confidentially and free of charge on this site and synchronize it with your own data so that others (your secretary or work colleagues) can see your schedule if you share a password and log-in.	www.anyday.com/	2	4

Sub Topic	Title	Description	URL	Rele-vance	Ease of Use
	Calendars Net	The site allows you to maintain calendars of events that are of interest to a group of people, free of charge. A link to Egroups (also in this section) lets you e-mail the group when new events are posted. Messy to look at, but a clever site from a public interest group in the US dedicated to improving communications and reducing global warming.	www.calendars.net/	3	2
	FreeDrive	FreeDrive gives you 20 Mb of free storage space so you can get access to your files from any Web terminal when away from your desk. Your data is password protected, but you'll have to pay $4.95 a month if you want secure encryption.	www.freedrive.com/	1	3
	e.groups	A cracking example of free services on the Internet. This one lets you maintain an e-mail list and bulletin board – really useful if you're working with distant colleagues or have a lot of relatives on e-mail. There's also a private chat room available if you're into that kind of thing.	www.egroups.com	2	4

GENERAL MARKETING

Sub Topic	Title	Description	URL	Rele-vance	Ease of Use
BASICS		Useful marketing information and related Internet tools that are worth becoming familiar with.			
	Amex Small Business Exchange	Whether or not you work in a small business the Amex Small Business Exchange is a network of sites covering essential business information. There is a soft sell of Amex services but also basic advice and beginners' guides. The marketing site includes helpful information on how to write a marketing plan, where to find services, how to buy mailing lists and lots more.	www6.americanexpress. com/smallbusiness/ segments/marketing. asp?aexp_nav= sbs_hp_id13	3	3

Sub Topic	Title	Description	URL	Rele-vance	Ease of Use
	Marketing UK	Excellent general site for the average marketing practitioner. Despite a slant towards IT, there are lots of useful lists and helpful links plus downloadable background information and reports. Clean simple design brings clarity.	www.marketinguk. co.uk/	2	3
	Marketing Magic	Free UK-based site that offers a range of tips, links and background reading, maintained as a very soft sell by a marketing consultancy in York. Provides links to recommended books that can be ordered via the site, which has an easy, accessible feel. Take a look at the business mentor service to see how the Net can help support small businesses.	www.tka.co.uk/magic	2	3
	Strathclyde University Business Information on the Internet	Comprehensive and independent round-up of online information, which is of value across all business disciplines and sectors. Mostly listings but some editorial. Not the prettiest site, but the search facility adds considerable value to both general and specialist enquiries.	www.dis.strath.ac.uk/ business/index.html	2	2
	A guide to search tools	Even with someone 'taking the slog out' of searching you'll need an understanding of how to find what you need online. This academic site is simple to use and comprehensive in its advice and lists of resources. It's no fun 'wading through' the Internet 'mire', so get acquainted now with the best search techniques.	www.mmu.ac.uk/h-ss/dic/main/search.htm	3	2

Sub Topic	Title	Description	URL	Rele-vance	Ease of Use
E-MAIL LISTS		E-mail is simple to use, popular with almost every Internet user and offers lots of potential marketing benefits.			
	eGroups	Not a bunch of spaced-out rave kids but one of the most valuable free resources currently available on the Net. Set up your own lists to use on your own site, use e-mail groups for networks of co-workers, subscribe to other people's lists, search archives, store data online…	www.egroups.com	3	3
	Mouse Tracks: the List of Marketing Lists	Although not easy to search and by no means compre-hensive, this list offers direct links into e-mail-based lists (not newsgroups) that you can join straight away.	nsns.com/Mouse Tracks/tloml.html	2	2
	Kim Bayne's Marketing Lists on the Net	Very straightforward listing service for online mailing lists, Webzines, discussion forums and more. Part of a network of sites maintained by a US new media consultant that can be accessed via her home page. No editorial but covers a broad spread.	www.wolfBayne. com/lists/	2	2
ORGAN-IZATIONS		Professional and business organizations.			
	Advertising Association	Not slick, but it does contain a very useful drop-down menu linking to all of the Association's members' sites. Other parts of the site contain very useful briefing papers, links and listings of events, but they're not easy to find.	www.adassoc.org.uk/	2	1

Sub Topic	Title	Description	URL	Rele-vance	Ease of Use
	CIM	The Chartered Institute of Marketing site has a clean and simple layout and offers a variety of resources and information for any marketing professional, whether a member of CIM or not. Some parts of the site, such as careers information, news, jobs and events are up to date and offer a service online. Other parts only offer contact details.	www.cim.co.uk	2	2
	American Marketing Association	The site of one of the largest North American marketing organizations offers plenty for the non-member, including access to the various journals published by AMA, which are heavyweight academic studies into marketing-related issues. Don't expect too much detailed UK information as we're 'lumped in' the region labelled Europe and Asia.	www.ama.org	2	2
	Business Link UK	Business Link provides support and resources for businesses through a regional network. The site contains details of what they do, contact numbers and clickable links to local offices, but little useful information is available online.	www.businesslink.co.uk/	1	1
EDUCATION AND TRAINING		Hone your skills, pick some top tips, share ideas with other marketers.			
	Market Files	Case studies from around the world, many of which can be viewed for free (for the time being, it says). Payment secures full reports but the site still offers useful background reading that gives insight into strategy and tactics from a range of sectors, and it has a distinctly international flavour.	www.marketfiles.net/	2	2

Sub Topic	Title	Description	URL	Rele-vance	Ease of Use
	Net Academy	Heavyweight site spanning a range of scientific interests, maintained by the Institute for Media and Communications Management, University of St.Gallen, Switzerland. The Business Media section is a stimulating mixture of theory, practice and future-gazing about the new business environments being created online.	www.businessmedia.org/businessmedia/businessmedia.nsf/whatsnew?ReadForm	2	2
	Advertising Association	A variety of background papers, student briefings and industry news is held in the Association's library, and it seems some of it has made it online. Useful information to get going, links to materials published elsewhere, helpful contacts and an industry overview. Not wonderful but mostly competent, with a useful drop-down menu on the home page listing other professional bodies.	www.adassoc.org.uk/inform/content.html	1	1
	Institute of Direct Marketing	Like many of the professional institute efforts, this is a good-looking 'corporate brochure' style site that contains very little other than details of the IDM's own courses. In this case this is tolerable as the details are well laid out, clearly explained and cover almost every aspect of direct marketing. Offers the bonus of an online booking facility.	www.theidm.co.uk	2	2
MARKETING SERVICES		Links to suppliers.			

Sub Topic	Title	Description	URL	Rele-vance	Ease of Use
	Marketing and Creative Handbook	It's all a bit clunky but this is the Web site version of a printed directory of UK marketing-related businesses. Full range of information but not fully Web-enabled, and essentially a cut-down version that tries to sell the print product.	www.mch.co.uk/	1	1
	elateral	A glimpse of the future at the range of marketing services that will be delivered online. Elateral provides fully customizable sales literature for any business using channel marketing techniques. Sophisticated software enables distributors and resellers to log on from anywhere in the world, customize their literature and order print runs. Check out the demo.	www.elateral.com/	3	3
TENDERS		Keep tabs on big contracts that are out to tender.			
Tenders	Tenders on The Web	EU rules dictate that all public sector contracts over 200,000 euros should be open to tender. This specialist UK-based site collates and publishes information about contracts and sells reports that can be viewed online. Includes news facility.	www.tenders.co.uk	2	1
ADVERTISING					
RESOURCES		Information about and for the advertising industry.			
	Below The Line Debrief	Searchable content culled from a range of sources, including the FT and other national dailies, national weeklies, marketing titles and elsewhere. The dossier feature helps you collect information as you trawl through extensive archives.	www.debrief.co.uk/	2	2

Sub Topic	Title	Description	URL	Rele-vance	Ease of Use
	About.com	Despite its US-centric view of the world this is a useful site for finding a range of global advertising-related resources. About.com uses specialist guides to bring a personal touch to its reviews and listings and also has helpful background information, as well as reporting industry news.	advertising.about.com/	1	2
MEDIA LISTS		Search for specific titles online, or review a particular industry.			
	Media UK	Links to UK media sites available through searches as well as clickable maps. Programming details for main terrestrial channels and Web links to a host of related resources. Excellent first point of call when looking for basic information.	www.mediauk.com/directory/	2	3
	Magazine.net	The Periodical Publishers Association maintains a variety of resources for those in the publishing industry, including a list of over 200 magazine titles available online. No search mechanism but the format is simple with Web links grouped under subject headings.	www.ppa.co.uk/fun.htm	2	2
	Adweb	Commercial site offering design and hosting services, which includes simple, well-maintained listings available through drop-down menus. Also available are sections such as TV, radio, advertising agencies, press, and UK information is mixed with international links. A simple but effective round-up.	www.adweb.co.uk/	1	2

Sub Topic	Title	Description	URL	Rele-vance	Ease of Use
MEDIA RESEARCH		Get background information about the media covering a particular area.			
	JICREG Listings	The Joint Industry Committee for Regional Press Research publishes detailed data about regional newspapers. This very simple site provides direct online access to demographic and circulation data, which is updated twice a year. Much more than just a list of titles.	www.jicreg.co.uk/	3	2
	MapMedia	This commercial site offers an online ordering service to map media for any area in the UK. It currently provides detailed readership information based on postcodes or other geographical groupings, including drive-time areas. Set up an account or pay online.	www.mapmedia.co.uk/	2	2
AD AGENCIES		Check out agencies online, but don't be surprised by the well-polished hard sell.			
	Institute of Practitioners in Advertising	Members listing for one of the largest UK professional associations. Useful clickable map and Web links in search results. Can be used to find agencies by location or name, and has other helpful resources on the site.	www.ipa.co.uk/contents/	2	2
NEWS		Advertising-related news.			
	Media Week	Basic site offering limited news and features taken from the print version, including opinions, international news and details of forthcoming features. Also has a link to a searchable database of advertising industry jobs through the People Bank.	www.mediaweek.co.uk	1	2

Sub Topic	Title	Description	URL	Rele-vance	Ease of Use
	MAD.CO.UK	Searchable, broad-ranging portal-style site, carrying news, features and listings in various 'channels'. Combines the information from 13 Centaur titles such as *Design Week*, *Marketing Week* and *Creative Review*. Registration and subscription required for services such as full archive searches and e-mail alerts, but there's plenty here for free.	www.mad.co.uk/ advertising/ad_ag/	2	3
	ChannelSeven	See what the offline titles are missing by using this network of sites to find up-to-date high-level commentary and news from the world of online marketing and advertising. It is US-biased but in a new global medium that's where the news is, so go get it!	www.channelseven .com/	3	3
	New Media Age	The graphics-laden site of the pre-eminent voice on the UK new media industry. Subscribers can access full stories from the weekly magazine, the searchable archives, a Web-site gallery, aggregated rate-card figures for the UK and lots more.	www.nma.co.uk/	2	2
ORGAN-IZATIONS		Official and professional bodies.			
	Institute of Practitioners in Advertising	Members listing for one of the largest UK professional associations. Useful clickable map and Web links in search results. Can be used to find agencies by location or name, and has other helpful resources on the site.	www.ipa.co.uk/contents/	2	2

Sub Topic	Title	Description	URL	Rele-vance	Ease of Use
	Advertising Standards Authority	Useful if you're looking for basic information about advertisers' legal responsibilities. Includes briefing papers, recent adjudications and an annual summary, which offers an insight into what happens when a complaint is made about an advertisement.	www.asa.org.uk/	1	1
	ISBA	The Incorporated Society of British Advertisers represents the interests of UK advertisers on numerous bodies, offers workshops, events and publications and has over 300 members. Valuable if you're one of them; otherwise it's no more than an advertisement for itself.	www.isba.org.uk	1	1
AUDITING		Online or off, who's reading what?			
	ABC	The Audit Bureau of Circulations provides a useful Web site for reading around the issues of auditing circulation and readership, with links to those UK publications registered with ABC and some statistics to browse for interest. Also has a new service for online publications, with samples and case studies. Payment is required to get detailed information and auditing services.	www.abc.org.uk	2	2

DIRECT MARKETING

RESOURCES		Useful information, news, tips, etc.			

Sub Topic	Title	Description	URL	Rele-vance	Ease of Use
	Direct Marketing Association	The UK-based DMA provides an excellent starting point for direct marketers looking for useful resources online. Some parts of the site are for DMA members only, but there's still lots of useful stuff for the casual surfer. This includes background material, advice, best practice guidelines, case studies and lists of international associations. For reference rather than news but very useful.	www.dma.org.uk	3	3
	Direct Mail Information Service	DMIS produces reports on the effectiveness of direct mail and carries out surveys into various aspects of the business of direct marketing. The site includes only brief glimpses of the reports, but there is an e-mail service to notify you about new publications.	www.dmis.co.uk/	1	1
LISTS		Run queries, view results, buy lists, use lists. Sit still.			
	Yellow Pages Business Database	Minimalist design almost manages to conceal just how much is on offer here. A valu-able data source for anyone looking for lists or basic mailing data. At least as easy as buying the information anywhere else, but with the bonus of lots of useful stuff free.	www.yellowpages business.co.uk/ tbd/index.html	2	2
	Dun & Bradstreet	Online UK list buying made easy. Start by choosing your search criteria using tick boxes and simple-to-follow instructions and you'll be given a count of results. The process can be slightly longwinded if you want to make lots of refinements in terms of numbers, but you can order and pay for the list online, and an account will be set up for you to keep track of previous requests.	directmarketing. uk.dnb.com	4	3

Sub Topic	Title	Description	URL	Rele-vance	Ease of Use
INTER-NATIONAL		Links to direct marketing sites outside the UK.			
	Direct Magazine	Mainly US news but does have useful commentary and professional insight of general interest. International (ie non-US) information is useful although it's all a bit thin.	www.directmag.com/	1	2
	Federation of European Direct Marketing (FEDMA)	European network for direct marketing associations. Little to recommend the site if you're not involved with FEDMA, except a list of Web links for European direct marketing associations, and related sites worldwide.	www.fedma.org/ infosystem/index.html	1	1
GUIDES		What is direct marketing? Where does all the jargon come from?			
	Royal Mail	A natural interest in direct mail activities is reflected in the Royal Mail site for business users. Lots of useful background information, links to reports, advice and explanations of the relevant Royal Mail services. Not too much the average direct marketer doesn't already know, but it's a well-designed interactive site that even lets you buy stamps online.	www.royalmail.co.uk/ atwork/direct/	2	3
	Inside Direct Mail	Since it's generally the case that they invent the jargon, this American site is a good place to find a lexicon of the key words you'll need to use to be in with the DM (direct marketing) in-crowd. Forms part of a news site for US-based marketers that is less useful but could be worth a look.	www2.insidedirect mail.com/dmglossary. html	2	2

Sub Topic	Title	Description	URL	Rele-vance	Ease of Use
NEWS		Keep up to date with the direct marketing industry.			
	dm.news	US-based site with news about the direct marketing industry, with a particular slant towards Internet marketing. Includes all sorts of categories for news, advertisements and directories, which provide a useful mix of background information and ongoing debate about techniques and tactics.	www.dmnews.com	2	2
	Precision Marketing	As part of Centaur's MAD UK site, *Precision Marketing* offers both its own news and integrates with that of 12 other marketing-related titles. News and features straight from the print edition, plus jobs, commentary and even the letters. Link back to the MAD home page for an even fuller picture of what's happening in marketing.	www.mad.co.uk/PM	3	2
E-MAIL MARKETING		Are you using e-mail the way you use postal marketing? Why not?			
	Process Request	This is a promotional site for a commercial online service specializing in e-mail marketing activities. It's mentioned here because it offers lots of useful information about what works and what doesn't, as well as the odd shameless 'plug' for its own products (which presumably do work?)	www.process request.com	2	2

Sub Topic	Title	Description	URL	Rele-vance	Ease of Use
INTERNET MARKETING					
RESOURCES		Where to start looking. . .and what you're looking for.			
	Revolution	One of the glossy print titles concerned with new media marketing, now weekly in the UK. The site has news, background information, jobs and a directory of new media service providers to help you find the specialist you're looking for.	www.revolution. haynet.com	3	3
	Ad Resource	Listed elsewhere for specialist information, this US-based site has articles, listings and information of general value to anyone trying to come to terms with what marketing on the Internet is all about. Not a guide, just a straightforward and useful site, albeit with a slightly cluttered design.	www.adresource.com/	3	2
	Information Society Initiative	UK-government project to encourage businesses to make more effective use of new technology. Raises key issues about the use of IT within business and provides case studies, useful links and the latest benchmarking surveys. Useful round-up helps set the scene for the market in business to business online activity, but can seem a bit thin in places.	www.isi.gov.uk/isi/	2	2
	Articles on online marketing and advertising	A slightly overwhelming list of links with editorial, which covers an impressive spread of related issues. Has a global flavour but inevitably is biased towards US commentary and attitudes.	www.ntu.edu.sg/ library/adv/articles.htm	2	1

Sub Topic	Title	Description	URL	Rele-vance	Ease of Use
	I-Advertising	Web-based interactive messaging system that enables you to discuss online advertising issues with literally thousands of people. It takes a bit of a leap of faith to plunge into this sort of environment but this is a great way of seeing what problems other people are encountering, and what sorts of solutions are being suggested. Exploits the ability of the Net to promote peer group discussion in new ways.	www.internet advertising.org/ qa/faq.shtml	1	1
	The Internet Marketing Centre	US-based site that has a lot of very useful information, ideas, tips and links. Free monthly newsletter is delivered by e-mail and the whole thing has an air of authority, both as somewhere to get started and as somewhere to keep coming back to.	www.marketingtips. com/	2	2
NEWS		Who's doing what? Is it working? Why on earth not?			
	ChannelSeven. com	Collects news and links from a variety of related sites to provide an excellent resource for anyone looking for information, ideas and contacts for marketing online. Newsletter available by e-mail, comprehensive background information and much more.	www.channel seven.com/	3	2
	Internet Works Magazine	A UK print magazine that combines a reasonable level of technical information with features and information on business applications and reviews of relevant products. Bridges the technology/ marketing divide and interprets the jargon for both. Offline subscription available through the site.	www.iwks.com	3	3

The Top 200 Web sites for marketing

Sub Topic	Title	Description	URL	Rele-vance	Ease of Use
	Online Marketing	Online section from *Marketing* magazine. Mostly under-whelming as it's a single page with a few news stories, fewer links and not much else.	www.marketing. haynet.com/ online/online.html	1	1
WHO'S ONLINE?		A basic question for any marketer, along with 'What are they doing there?'.			
	NUA Surveys	Long-standing Internet-only survey company. Based in Ireland, it compiles results from a variety of sources on a rolling basis. Search the Web site for all sorts of goodies, and try the excellent mailing lists to keep a finger on the Internet's pulse.	www.nua.ie/surveys/	4	2
	CyberAtlas	US-based global perspective on the geographics, demographics and behaviour of Internet usage. Provides useful news and background information, as well as a range of statistics from a variety of sources. Newsletter can keep you up to date with what's going on.	cyberatlas. internet.com	2	2
ONLINE STRATEGY		New technology brings new challenges and new rules of engagement to learn.			
	Net Marketing	Not all sites are as US-centric as this, but it does have an excellent range of information, ideas and examples. Predominantly concerned with business to business marketing it includes a chance to peruse its suggested 'Top 200 b2b' (lovely jargon) sites.	www.netb2b.com/	2	1

Sub Topic	Title	Description	URL	Rele-vance	Ease of Use
	High Tech Advertising White Papers	Articles written by someone who not only knows his or her way around marketing online but also has a good turn of phrase to help keep things very readable. They're too long to digest online but they're easily printed.	www.pawluk. com/pages/ marketingj.shtml	3	2
	Target Marketing	Jim Sterne is a US author and commentator who regularly adds wise words to the pile of hyperbole that surrounds the Internet. This site lists articles he's written and it makes a very stimulating base for a 'quick dip'. His recent books peel back the layers of technology to reveal the marketing basics beneath.	www.targeting.com/ articles-date.html	3	2
INTERNET ADVERTISING		Get to grips with banner ads, click-though rates and counting eyeballs.			
	Ad Resources	US site that sifts through various issues of concern to anyone buying advertising online. This part of the sprawling network of sites that form Internet.com collects stories from many sources. An excellent overview of key areas.	adres.internet.com/	3	2
	Internet Advertising Resource Centre	Worth a trawl for news, links, contacts and background information, mostly focused on Internet advertising, but of wider interest to anyone marketing online. It grew out of academic research and is maintained at Michigan State University, but also lists commercial services and accepts advertising.	www.admedia.org/	2	2

Sub Topic	Title	Description	URL	Rele-vance	Ease of Use
	Internet Advertising Bureau	The US bias to events and news may not be useful to many people, but the background reading on this site provides insight on a rapidly changing industry. IAB is a not-for-profit organization and its site has press releases, articles and links to tools for managing your online advertising activities.	www.iab.net/advertise/adsource.html	2	2
MARKETING YOUR SITE		How to get more of the people you want visiting your site.			
	Link Exchange	A Microsoft-owned site that collects together a number of valuable online resources for starting, promoting and managing your Web site. It's a cluttered portal offering a range of services – submitting your site to up to 200 search engines at one time, an inspection of your site and several tactics for attracting more of the visitors you want to your Web pages. A few things are free, everything else fairly cheap, especially if it keeps the eyeballs coming.	www.linkexchange.com/	3	2
	Emarketer	A news and information site about online marketing. Facts and figures have a distinctly North American flavour and you'll have to pay for full market reports. But keeping tabs on what's going on over there may be very useful in keeping people visiting your site over here.	www.emarketer.com/	2	2
	Site Sell	A straightforwardly commercial site from someone with a book to sell about how you convert Web sites into real sales. One amongst many but has lots to offer for free – implementing one of his own tips – and worth a look if only as a case study for small sites.	www.sitesell.com/	2	1

Sub Topic	Title	Description	URL	Rele-vance	Ease of Use
	Marketing Resources info Center	You don't have to look far for lists of sites that will help promote your site. At least this one is both short and contains editorial. It also places value on services that are free, so worth a look when you're not sure how much you want to spend.	www.marketing resource.com/	1	1
AUDITING		Which sites are getting the eyeballs?			
	ABC// Electronic	Headline data is free on this site, which is the online arm of the Audit Bureau of Circulations. As traditional media tools shift to cater for the online world this a good site for background information. You see the data for key sites and buy services from ABC to audit your own site.	www.abc.org.uk/ electronic	2	2

INTERNATIONAL MARKETING

Sub Topic	Title	Description	URL	Rele-vance	Ease of Use
NEWS		Keep up to date with news elsewhere.			
	Kidon Media Link	There's nothing fancy about this listing service maintained in Holland. Simple structure, basic categories, lists media titles by country, provides Web links. Easy!	www.dds.nl/ kidon/ media-link/	2	2
	CNN Financial News	You'll be watching it in the hotel room when you get there, so why not check out the Web site for the same high-quality round-up of international news? Occasional gripes about US bias aside this is as comprehensive as you'd expect, with a financial news site alongside other specialist sections.	cnnfn.com/	3	3

Sub Topic	Title	Description	URL	Rele-vance	Ease of Use
	Foreign and Commonwealth Office	The excellent Foreign and Commonwealth Office site links to several other trade sites, whether promoting inward investment into the UK, or encouraging export activity. There is a lot of useful reference material, as well as advice on travelling to specific locations. The travel information can be personalized and e-mail sent to advise on changing situations.	www.fco.gov.uk/ travel/default.asp	4	3
	Financial Times	The FT's regular market reports provide information on countries and informs on opportunities for export within certain sectors. The world news section has a business bias and the search mechanism enables you to pull out relevant stories about particular countries, which may be free to view or may require payment. Excellent.	www.ft.com	4	3
RESEARCH		Track down information about potential new markets. If you want to get to them, check Business essentials – Travel.			
	RBA Information Services	RBA offers training in the use of the Internet as a research tool and this page offers an overview of how to set about gathering international data. Very accessible style with useful links and tips to get you started.	www.rba.co.uk/sources/ country.htm	3	1
	UK Government Statistics Service	This site lists government statistical services in other countries – this may be useful for basic information, although there is no editorial or recommendation on the site to help guide you. Of course there is a disclaimer.	www.statistics.gov. uk/links/links.htm	1	1

Sub Topic	Title	Description	URL	Rele-vance	Ease of Use
EUROPE		Are you up to date with the single market and the introduction of the euro?			
	European Access	A site that helps to make sense of the myriad rules, regulations and opportunities in the European market. Good search facilities, a news service, publications and plenty of links make it a good all-purpose starting point. Due to be upgraded in the near future.	www.european access.co.uk/	2	2
	Europe in Prospect	Newsletter from International law firm Clifford Chance provides helpful information on a limited basis about legal matters in the EU. Site also links into their ongoing work across the world.	www.clifford chance.com/library/ newsletters/europrosp/ index.html	1	1
	Get Ready For the Euro	UK-government site combines propaganda for European Monetary Union with news and information about the impact of the euro on UK businesses. Good simple information but feels a bit thin. Use the links to find out how other countries are preparing for the new currency.	www.euro.gov.uk	2	1
	Euro Info Centre	EU-funded network of information centres provide a one-stop service for businesses. Modest site offers regular newsletter published online, as well as advertising business opportunities with partners from other EU states.	euro-info.org.uk/	2	1
SELLING ABROAD		Information, ideas, contacts for anyone looking to sell abroad. If foreign languages are a problem, see if the translation sites in Business essentials help.			

Sub Topic	Title	Description	URL	Rele-vance	Ease of Use
	International Trading Channel	This site incorporates Trade UK, which provides a matching service enabling UK businesses to find international business partners. Links into a number of online services within the Yellow Pages group. Still at its early stages, its usefulness will depend on its ability to build a global profile and attract visitors.	www.yellowpages business.co.uk/ international.html	1	1
	Export Today	US-based site but is, by definition, outward looking, so a lot of content and information is useful to UK marketers. Editorial and information from a print-based title.	www.exporttoday.com	1	1
	British Trade International	UK-government site for UK-based exporters forms a comprehensive online base for the promotion of British business overseas. Excellent resource with country reports, events listings by sector, links to other government offices, useful contacts and export-related news.	www.brittrade.com/	4	3
	1001 Sites – Arab World Online	All sorts of information from the Arab world, stretching from Algeria to the Yemen. Links to country information, news from various Middle Eastern sources and a searchable business directory. Not comprehensive but offers a different angle to official sources of information.	www.1001sites.com/	1	1
	UK Now – Japan	This is 'the British Government's official site in Japan', which has been set up to encourage and promote trade links between the UK and Japan. Includes news, useful information for visiting business people and helpful links, in both English and Japanese. Just one of the many useful sites that can be accessed through the Foreign and Commonwealth Office site.	www.uknow.or.jp/	2	3

Sub Topic	Title	Description	URL	Rele- vance	Ease of Use
	Foreign and Commonwealth Office	Useful for general travel advice, but also a rich seam to tap for all sorts of export-related information, linking to country information, international news, information on export licences and more. Don't leave home without checking here first.	www.fco.gov.uk/ trade/	4	3
	The Institute of Export	Information, links and news for members and others from the UK Institute of Export. Worth tracking down the news, which is somewhat hidden away in the Members Lounge, currently open to non-members. Lots of useful snippets of advice and contacts along the way.	www.export.org.uk/	2	2
INTER-NATIONAL LAW		How does the legal framework affect your ideas for export?			
	The World Law Guide	Want to see a copy of Chinese Patent Legislation? Uncertain about the inner workings of the Constitutional Court of Spain? Slightly creaky site appears to include broken links but could set you on the right path if things get serious.	www.lexadin.nl/ wlg/legis/nofr/ legis.htm	1	1

MARKETING RESEARCH

RESOURCES		Looking for somewhere online to help with your research activities? The IT sector is best represented but other information is available.			
	An Internet tour for Market Research	Straightforward introduction to how the Internet can be used for market research. Written by a UK-based academic, it avoids the trap of overwhelming the reader with links and concentrates on a few good examples for each of the methods discussed.	www.researchinfo. com/library/bradlen/ index.shtml	3	2

Sub Topic	Title	Description	URL	Rele-vance	Ease of Use
	Search Skills for Online Market Research	A chapter from a book published in the US that explains how to hone your search methods to avoid wasting your time online. Good basic introduction and some useful lists of US links elsewhere on the site, but not too much 'How To' because you're meant to buy the book!	www.vivamus. com/chap5.html	2	1
	RBA Information Services	Karen Blakeman of RBA provides training in this field and this is a helpful digest of advice for anyone carrying out business-related research online. Despite advising that free data is hard to find she offers a helpful overview and useful links. 'Dig around' the site for other lists and links to resources.	www.rba.co.uk/ sources/stats.htm	3	1
	Dun and Bradstreet	Business surveys and company information for the UK, searchable and free for basic information. There is an online payment option to obtain detailed information.	www.uk.dnb.com	3	3
	Market Research Society (MRS)	Useful introduction to what market research is, how it works and what it can do for you. But beyond that it's a bit of a disappointment: no lists of members, lots of order forms for MRS publications and not much useful content.	www.market research.org.uk/	1	1
	NOP UK	Limited access to survey results across a range of specialist areas, although the format for listing of articles is not simple, to say the least. Useful basic information is freely available and can be used to set you on the right path to buying what you really need.	www.nop.co.uk/ survey/department_ frame.htm	2	2

Sub Topic	Title	Description	URL	Rele- vance	Ease of Use
	Audit Bureau of Circulations	Searchable data for all newspapers and magazines that use ABC to audit their circulation figures. Free information is readily available for comparative purposes, once registered. If you subscribe you can see still more. Also has services for online publications called ABC/Electronic.	www.abc.org.uk	2	2
	The Economist Intelligence Unit	Comprehensive global information across wide range of sectors. You must register and enter credit card details to get access to the content of any reports, although a straightforward search facility means you can see whether it's there first.	store.eiu.com/	3	1
	UK Government Statistical Service	Review detailed statistics published by the UK Government. Some collated on a regional basis, some covering areas such as the economy, population, etc. Not very up to date by the standards of commercial services, but could provide a very broad-brush starting point.	www.statistics.gov.uk/ stats/ukinfigs/ukinfig .htm	2	1
	Office for National Statistics	Government site offers access to information from the Census and a variety of other official sources. Links to other government sites, including Statsbase, which can deliver all sorts of detailed data in a format compatible with most spreadsheets. You need to know what you're looking for, but it could well be here.	www.ons.gov.uk/	3	1

Sub Topic	Title	Description	URL	Rele-vance	Ease of Use
	The National Readership Survey	Want to know which magazines and newspapers are read by the most people? Topline information is free, giving helpful overviews of particular sectors. Serious data-miners can buy the information and analyse it on their own computer.	www.nrs.co.uk/ contents.cfm	2	1
	Durlacher	UK company specializing in research and consultancy across new media and technology sectors worldwide. Provides a range of reports available to buy, and plenty of sample reports for background reading on a number of marketing-related issues.	www.durlacher.com fr-research-reps.htm	3	2
COMPANY INFORMATION		Use the Net to trawl for information on competitors, prospects, partners or creditworthiness.			
	ICC Information	ICC offers a number of services using data collated from Companies House. The site includes samples of reports, clear pricing details and direct access to its services. Focuses on the needs of the City, but services are also valuable to those with lesser needs.	www.icc.co.uk/	2	2
	CAROL	A set of over 3000 company reports from large companies in the UK, Asia and Europe. Registration is free to companies, but coverage can be patchy. You are transferred to the company's Web site, so reports are not in a standard format.	www.carol.co.uk/	3	2

Sub Topic	Title	Description	URL	Rele-vance	Ease of Use
	Yell	Yell is the online service of the Yellow Pages. It draws on the business information in the printed pages to offer a fully searchable database of UK businesses, which can be used to find information by company type, company name or location. Very useful in general but could also help you uncover rivals, whether local or not.	www.yell.co.uk	3	3
	Kompass UK	Searchable online database that offers telephone numbers for free, with much more detailed mailing information available once an account is set up. Simple to use but let down by lack of information about cost of services.	www.kompass.co.uk	2	2
AGENCIES		Looking for a market research agency? These sites will go some way towards finding the right one for you.			
	Marketing Week	A straightforward searchable database of UK market research agencies. No frills and easy to use. An excellent place to start if you're looking for an agency and don't know where to begin. Search results include e-mail as well as Web links.	195.112.52.192/ rdirectory.htm	2	2
	Yell	This won't tell you much about what they can do but it is a comprehensive listing service of UK businesses with links to Web sites and into lists of related business types.	www.yell.co.uk/	2	2

Sub Topic	Title	Description	URL	Rele-vance	Ease of Use
	British Market Research Association	Offers full list of members with Web and e-mail links, but is not searchable and provides only contact details. BRMA does offer a service to help choose an agency, called SelectLine, but it's not available online.	www.bmra.org.uk	1	1
	ESOMAR	The European Society for Opinion and Market Research provides a forum for market research organizations from around the world. Its full directory is available online, with Web links, along with plenty of background materials about the industry.	www.esomar.nl/ countries/directory_ uk.html	2	2
PUBLIC RELATIONS					
BASICS		What is PR? What can I use it for? How does it work?			
	PR Web	US-based site but the PR Coach link has useful articles posted by PR practitioners.	prweb.com/ prcoach.htm	2	1
	What is Public Relations?	Straightforward guide to the main whys, whats and wherefores of PR.	www.pr-school-london.com/Resource/ WhatisPR.html	2	1
RESOURCES		An overview of what's going on in PR.			
	PR Consultants Association	Competent site includes jobs link service (with testimonials), lists of members with links to their Web pages, and access to latest news. Bit dry but functional.	www.martex. co.uk/prca/	2	1
	Communicators in Business	'No thrills' site for those in the business communications game. Useful lists of freelancers, news snippets and an events diary, but just one feature a month from the magazine seems a bit stingy.	www.bacb.org/	2	1

Sub Topic	Title	Description	URL	Rele-vance	Ease of Use
	PR Place	Heavy US bias but simple listings of various resources, including media lists, ideas for finding online links to journalists, and links to online news sources. UK information patchy and of only general value as a starting point.	www.prplace.com	1	1
AGENCY SERVICES		Whether you handle your own PR or use an agency these sites get your releases to journalists.			
	PR Net	Well-designed site that brings together those submitting press releases with those seeking news. Paid-for subscription services enable your releases to hit the desktops of wired newshounds worldwide.	www.prnet.co.uk/	2	3
	Internet Press Centre	Contact IT journalists easily using this paid-for online service. Submit your details online for a quote, pay up, then start mailing your press releases into the relevant hacks' in-trays.	www.internet presscentre.com/	1	1
NEWS		Keep track of changes in the heady world of PR.			
	PR Week	Keep up to date with news, jobs, and appointments in the PR industry. With links to sites for Asia and US editions.	www.prweekuk.com/ uk/homeindex.htm	1	1
	PA News Centre	Use this Press Association site to check headlines, read stories and receive daily news bulletin by e-mail in order to keep on top of things. You can even link their news into your own site.	www.pa.press.net/	2	2

Sub Topic	Title	Description	URL	Rele-vance	Ease of Use
	PR Newswire Europe News Network	Well-ordered site offers links to press releases as they hit the news wires, plus links to useful resources. Has PR Newswire sister site in US.	releases.twoten.press.net/		

NEWS AND MAGAZINES

Sub Topic	Title	Description	URL	Rele-vance	Ease of Use
BUSINESS NEWS		News about business to help you keep tabs on the bigger picture			
	Financial Times	The great strength of this site is its depth across a range of business-related information. Requires registration up front and the information services are slowly but surely being charged for. A lot remains free, however, with a comprehensive search tool making access easy. Information services can be paid for online to create an excellent business research tool.	www.ft.com/	4	3
	Business Wire	US-based site that provides access to a wide range of sector-specific news and information. Good for keeping tabs on global economic changes and what the big players are up to.	www.businesswire.com/	2	2
	News Now	Headline-driven site links to a variety of worldwide news sources and is updated every five minutes. Sorts stories into a range of headings and indicates country of origin to aid search. An ideal way of putting all sorts of up-to-date information at your fingertips.	www.newsnow.co.uk/	3	2

Sub Topic	Title	Description	URL	Rele-vance	Ease of Use
	BBC Business News	The BBC Web site is a network of high-quality news and information services and is reputed to be the most visited UK-based Web site. Headlines, market and company information are updated regularly. Features and discussion forums highlight issues of general concern to the business community. By no means a specialist resource, but it provides a good general overview.	news.bbc.co.uk/ hi/english/business/ default.htm	2	3
FINANCIAL NEWS		Keep track of dealings on the stock exchanges of the world			
	Bloomberg	Focuses on market information from the world's stock markets with a site for each of the main financial centres. Forms part of an international network of useful sites that includes personal as well as corporate finance. Subscription services provide access to more detailed stock information.	www.bloomberg. com/uk/	3	2
	TheStreet.com	Mixture of free stories and items marked Premium that you have to subscribe and pay for. A lively (and free) discussion forum collects reader responses to articles. US-focused but has a sister site at www.thestreet.co.uk.	www.thestreet.com/	1	2
	London Stock Exchange	A good starting point for tracking down information and news about activity on the London Stock Exchange. Includes a variety of helpful guides to using information, a useful list of related sites, lists of companies trading and more. And it's all free!	www.london stockex.co.uk/	2	3

Sub Topic	Title	Description	URL	Rele- vance	Ease of Use
	NASDAQ	Comprehensive online services seamlessly integrated with activity on the Exchange itself as well as AMEX and Hong Kong markets. Prices, news and company information available easily, plus analysis and other features. Complex if you're unfamiliar with the market, essential if you're either quoted or investing.	www.nasdaq.com/	3	3
MARKETING NEWS		Want to keep abreast of who's doing what in the marketing industry?			
	MAD UK	This UK-based portal-style site draws its content from 13 Centaur-owned titles, including *Marketing Week, Precision Marketing* and *Creative Review*. Mixes up stories, provides access to the latest online versions of each and has an excellent search facility. A Web site that comprehensively adds up to more than the sum of its parts.	www.mad.co.uk/	4	2
	Marketing	Online version of the print magazine, with a very slender one-page extra about the new media marketing business. The site has all the regular bits from the weekly magazine, along with video versions in the Adwatch section and a few interactive features. Nothing special but usual high-quality editorial.	www.marketing. haynet.com/	3	3

Sub Topic	Title	Description	URL	Rele-vance	Ease of Use
	Yahoo! News	The Yahoo! news facility allows you to use any search term you wish, but the results are not as focused as a marketing-specific news site. Worth trying as a general news facility that can sometimes throw up useful snippets, which are gleaned from other sources. Try adding something about your own sector to narrow it down a bit.	search.news.yahoo. com/search/news?p =marketing+UK	1	2
	Sales and Marketing Management	It has a strong North American flavour but some of the ideas and background reading will be stimulating to anyone grappling with management issues. Subscribers to the print magazine can access the archives but what you can get for free makes it worth a quick look now and then.	www.salesand marketing.com/	1	2
	Brand Week	US-based review of all things marketing sits alongside the *Media Week* sister site. There's not much UK information here, but this straightforward news site will keep up to date with international marketing news and it also features an e-mail news service. Full use of the search facilities requires a subscription plus a small per-report payment.	www.brand week.com/	2	2
CONSUMER AFFAIRS		UK and European resources on consumer rights and consumer issues.			
	Office of Fair Trading	Well-organized site with useful advice about knowing your rights, and information about how to complain.	www.oft.gov.uk/	2	1

Sub Topic	Title	Description	URL	Rele-vance	Ease of Use
	EU DGXXIV Consumer Voice	Heavyweight to the point of 'stodgy' site for Europe-wide consumer policy and consumer health protection, maintained from Brussels in three languages. Download copies of the quarterly consumer-voice newsletter, check press releases and use the library to access legislation, reports and surveys.	europa.eu.int/ comm/dg24/library/ pub/cv/index_en.html	2	1
MEDIA LISTS		Links to current titles published online.			
	Newsdirectory .com	US-based site linking to international media titles in a range of categories. Tends to have an IT bias but integrates the data across the site in a number of useful ways. Worth visiting the home page too.	www.newsdirectory .com./news/magazine/ business/salesmkt/	1	2

EVENTS AND CONFERENCES

Sub Topic	Title	Description	URL	Rele-vance	Ease of Use
RESOURCES		Opportunities to discuss, sell or show.			
	Trade Fairs and Exhibitions UK	Exhaustive listings of trade exhibitions and related events searchable by date, type, venue and organizer. The disappointing listings format doesn't include Web links.	www.exhibitions.co.uk/	2	1
	AMEX Trade Show Info	Global information about events across a bewildering range of sectors. Searchable by date, city, sector or name of the show, with Web links and other clickable information. Excellent resource for US information, but patchy elsewhere, depending on sector.	www.tsnn.com/ bclass/amex/ marketing.htm		

Sub Topic	Title	Description	URL	Rele-vance	Ease of Use
	Economist Intelligence Unit	A global leader in senior level conferences, hosted in venues in many different countries. The site lists forthcoming events and details of each, but there is no booking capability.	www.economist conferences.com	1	1
	The Biz	The UK-based Business Information Zone provides a wide range of useful online services, including this database of forthcoming events. Searchable by sector, venue, date and other criteria, with Web links for the results.	www.thebiz.co.uk/ eventscalendar.asp	2	2
MARKETING EVENTS		Events of interest to marketing professionals.			
	Advertising Association	Not slick or pretty, but this site has the virtue of being up to date and it contains a listing of various marketing-related events on the horizon. Provides e-mail contacts for further details, but no Web link. Search function located through home page.	www.adassoc.org. uk/events.html	2	1

Index

1-to-1 Web Site 43–44
A2B Travel 52
ad agencies sites 90
advanced users 82–83
Advertising Association 68
advertising sites 35–39, 88–92,
    99–100
Adweb 38
affiliate schemes 59
agencies sites 109–10
agency selection 35–36
agency services sites 111
Amazon.com 55–56, 59
American Express 31, 67
Anchordesk 65, 66
Audit Bureau of Circulations
    39, 72, 73
auditing sites 92, 101

Babelfish 48–49
BBC Business News site 63

benefits of the Internet 9–10
biz, the 67
British Airways miniguides 50,
    51
British Trade International 50
'business essentials' sites 8,
    77–83
business information sites
    77–78
business news sites 112–13

Campaign 67, 72
Channel Seven 37, 56
chinwag 61
'cluttered portal' sites 17–18
CNNfn site 46
commercial sites 12–13
company information sites
    108–09
conference information sites
    66–69, 116–17

consumer affairs sites   115–16
'corporate brochure' sites   13,
    14–15
'cunningly concealed
    commercial' sites   18–19

deja.com   28
direct marketing   40–45, 92–95
Direct Marketing Association
    34
directories   13
DIY marketing advice   31–33
dmnews.com   44
'dull but worthy' sites   19–20,
    33–34
Dun and Bradstreet   42–43, 45,
    71
Durlacher   71, 72

'ease of use' criterion   3, 4, 5
Economic Intelligence Unit   71
Economist Conferences, The
    68, 69
education sites   86–87
egg.com   55–56
e-mail   22–27, 65
e-mail lists   85
e-mail marketing sites   95
Euro Info Centre   52, 53
European marketing sites
    103–05
European Union sites   52–53
events information sites   66–69,
    116–17

financial news sites   113–14
Financial Times   46, 47, 64
'firm favourite' sites   20–21
'flashy Flash' sites   16–17
Foreign and Commonwealth
    Office   47, 48
free e-mail   26
free information   10–11
ft.com   46, 47, 64

general marketing sites   83–88,
    30–35
Get Ready for the Euro site   53
guides lists   94

Illustra Research   3
'information jungle'   7–8
Institute of Export   50
Institute of Practitioners of
    Advertising (IPA)   35–36
international direct marketing
    sites   94
international marketing sites
    45–53, 101–05
Internet advertising sites
    99–100
Internet marketing sites   54–62,
    96–101
IPA, *see* Institute of Practitioners
    of Advertising

Kidon Media Link   48

'labour of love' sites   15–16

legal sites   82
lists sites   45, 62, 93

mad.co.uk   36–37
magazines sites   63–66, 112–16
many-to-many e-mail   27
Map Media   39
marketfiles.net   34
Marketing   72
Marketing Magic   32
marketing new sites   114–15
marketing research sites   70–73,
    105–10
marketing services sites   87–88
Marketing UK   33, 60
Marketing Week   67, 72
'marketing your site' sites
    100–01
media lists sites   89–90, 116
media sites   80–81
Media UK   38
Media Week   72
money information sites   82
Mouse Tracks   62
multi-level marketers   55
Multimap   21, 51, 52

Net Academy on Business
    Media   35
Net Marketing   60
New Media Age   37
news sites   17–18, 63–69, 80–81,
    112–16
    advertising   90–91

direct marketing   95
international marketing
    101–02
Internet marketing   97–98
    public relations   111–12
newsgroups   27–29
Nua Surveys   57, 58, 66

one-to-many e-mail   24
one-to-one e-mail   23–24
organizations, sites of
    trade/professional   33–35,
    85, 91–92

'portal' sites   17–18
post information sites   79–80
Precision Marketing   44
Prnet   75–76
professional organization sites
    33–35, 85, 91–92
public-relations sites   74–76,
    110–12
pyramid sellers   55

rating sites   3–6
RBA Information Services   49,
    73
registration forms   59
relevance criterion   3, 4, 5
research sites   102, 105–10
resources sites   30–35
    advertising   88–89
    direct marketing   92–93
    events and occurrences
    116–17

Internet marketing   96–97
  public relations   110–11
Revolution   56
Royal Mail   41

search engines   7
selecting sites   3–6
Small Business Exchange
  (American Express)   31, 67
'spam'   24–25
star ratings   5–6
strategy sites   98–99

Target Marketing   58
telephone information sites
  79–80
tenders sites   88
threshold criteria, establishing
  4
time information sites   79
Trade Fairs and Exhibitions UK
  site   68

trade organization sites   33–35,
  85, 91–92
training sites   86–87
travel sites   78–79
types of sites   14–21

UK National Readership Survey
  72
user-driven basis of guide   9
'user' general guidelines   7–13

value of the Internet   8–9
vendors   12–13
visitor data   59

weather information sites   79
'who's online?' sites   98
writing aids sites   81–82

Yellow Pages   41–42, 45

ZDNet   65, 66

About Illustra Research

Illustra Research was formed in January 1999 to develop products and services that would make the Internet more effective and easier to use for everyone. Their mission is to put the power of the Internet within easy reach of both novice and experienced users alike.

Located in the Sussex Innovation Centre at the University of Sussex, UK, it is supported by a network of specialists and experts in the UK and the USA who cooperate on specific projects, using the Internet as a collaborative tool. Illustra also employs teams of researchers who surf the Web to locate relevant material. They are managed by Web Editors, who work alongside subject specialists to rigorously evaluate information according to a unique methodology.

The directors of Illustra :

Alan Saunders, Managing Director, has been in the multimedia industry since its birth and has worked on projects for a wide range of blue-chip clients including Hewlett Packard, Olivetti, British Airways, NEC and Panasonic.

Colin Dixon, Technical Director, has worked with computer networking systems and PC technologies for over 15 years.

Alan Cawson, Research Director, is Professor of Digital Media and Director of the Digital Media Research Centre at the University of Sussex. He has been involved with the Web since its birth in 1993, and writes extensively on consumer information technologies.

For further information about Illustra's activities please contact:

Illustra Research Limited
The Sussex Innovation Centre
Science Park Square
Falmer
Brighton BN1 9SB
Tel: 01273 234650
e-mail: info@illustra-net.com

How to Use Your Top 200 CD-ROM

The CD-ROM that accompanies this book runs under Windows 95, Windows 98 and Windows NT4.0. It is a combination of a high-quality information directory and a fully featured Web browser. The information directory is a guide to the Internet, in which relevant sites are identified, and ordered by topic and sub-topic. Each site has been evaluated for relevance and ease of use according to systematic criteria. Integrated with the directory is a Web browser engine, Microsoft's Internet Explorer, providing seamless integration with the Internet. The browser provides all online features of Internet Explorer, so the user is not 'missing' any functions available to users of other browsers.

1 Topic Index   One-click access to links organized within topics and sub-topics using drop-down menus which helps users move quickly to the subject area they wish to research.

2 Browser Window   The user sees entries in the directory in the browser window, and with a   single click can navigate to the relevant Internet site.

3 Toolbar   A clear toolbar provides one-click access to key functions, including Back, Forward and Print. A special 'Guide' button returns the user immediately to the directory — saving time and providing instant help when 'lost' on the Internet.

4 Menu Bar   A standard Windows Menu Bar contains all the functions of the CD-ROM.

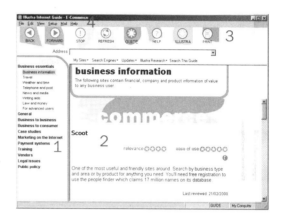

Installation

The CD-ROM installs easily on the user's hard disk. The user can choose where it is installed. Full uninstallation is provided.

Online Update

The Internet is changing all the time as sites appear, change or close down. The CD-ROM includes an update feature, through which users can connect directly to the Illustra Web site, and download an updated version in a matter of seconds.

System Requirements

PC System	Memory (RAM)	16 Mbytes minimum
	Disk Space	20 Mbytes required
	CD-ROM	4x required
	Operating System	Windows 95, Windows 98, Windows NT4.0 (Service Pack 3 or later)
Display	Minimum screen resolution	800x600
	Minimum screen colour depth	15-bit (32768 colours)
Online Requirements	Internet Connection	Windows dial-up or LAN connection to Internet provider
	Modem	Any supported Windows modem
	Microsoft Internet Explorer	Optional. The Guide will supply Internet Explorer functions where IE is not installed, and will upgrade IE versions 1–4 to IE5.